50 New Years Lunch Recipes for Home

By: Kelly Johnson

Table of Contents

- Classic Beef Wellington
- Lemon Herb Roasted Chicken
- Creamy Tomato Basil Soup
- Garlic Parmesan Stuffed Mushrooms
- Spinach Artichoke Dip with Crostini
- Chicken Marsala
- Stuffed Bell Peppers
- Baked Ziti with Italian Sausage
- Seafood Paella
- Vegetable Lasagna
- Pulled Pork Sliders
- Pesto Pasta Salad
- Mushroom Risotto
- Quiche Lorraine
- Buffalo Chicken Wings
- Beef Stroganoff
- Thai Green Curry
- Eggplant Parmesan
- Grilled Salmon with Avocado Salsa
- Chicken Fajitas
- Lentil Soup with Ham
- Crispy Pork Belly Tacos
- Butternut Squash Soup
- BBQ Chicken Pizza
- Vegetarian Chili
- Shrimp Scampi
- Sweet and Sour Meatballs
- Chicken Alfredo
- Cobb Salad
- Stuffed Acorn Squash
- Beef Tacos with Salsa Verde
- Greek Salad with Lemon Vinaigrette
- Salmon Cakes
- Roasted Beet and Goat Cheese Salad
- Chicken Parmesan
- Spaghetti Carbonara

- Cheese and Charcuterie Board
- Chicken and Waffles
- Pork Schnitzel
- Vegetable Stir-Fry
- Chicken Shawarma
- Cornbread and Chili Bake
- Grilled Portobello Mushrooms
- Buffalo Cauliflower Bites
- Pasta Primavera
- Honey Glazed Ham
- Baked Brie with Cranberries
- Roasted Vegetable Tart
- Beef and Broccoli Stir-Fry
- Cajun Shrimp and Grits

Classic Beef Wellington

Ingredients:

For the Beef:

- 2 pounds beef tenderloin (center-cut)
- 2 tablespoons olive oil
- Salt and freshly ground black pepper, to taste
- 2 tablespoons Dijon mustard

For the Duxelles:

- 1 pound mushrooms (such as cremini or button), finely chopped
- 2 tablespoons unsalted butter
- 1 small onion, finely chopped
- 2 cloves garlic, minced
- ¼ cup dry white wine
- 2 tablespoons fresh thyme leaves
- Salt and freshly ground black pepper, to taste

For Assembly:

- 8 slices prosciutto
- ½ pound pâté (optional, such as chicken liver or foie gras)
- 1 package (14 ounces) puff pastry, thawed
- 1 egg, beaten (for egg wash)

Instructions:

1. **Prepare the Beef:**
    - Preheat your oven to 400°F (200°C).
    - Season the beef tenderloin generously with salt and pepper.
    - In a large skillet, heat olive oil over high heat. Sear the beef on all sides until browned, about 2-3 minutes per side. Remove from heat and let cool.
    - Brush the beef with Dijon mustard and let it cool completely.
2. **Make the Duxelles:**
    - In the same skillet, melt the butter over medium heat. Add the onions and garlic and cook until softened, about 3-4 minutes.
    - Add the finely chopped mushrooms and cook until the moisture has evaporated and the mixture is dry, about 10 minutes.
    - Add the white wine and cook until the wine has evaporated. Stir in the thyme and season with salt and pepper. Let cool.
3. **Assemble the Wellington:**
    - On a lightly floured surface, roll out the puff pastry into a rectangle large enough to wrap around the beef.

- Lay out the prosciutto slices on the puff pastry, slightly overlapping them.
- Spread the cooled duxelles evenly over the prosciutto.
- If using pâté, spread a thin layer over the beef tenderloin.
- Place the cooled beef on top of the duxelles and prosciutto.
- Carefully roll the puff pastry around the beef, sealing the edges and making sure the seam is on the bottom. Trim any excess pastry.
- Brush the entire pastry with beaten egg.

4. **Bake:**
    - Place the wrapped beef on a baking sheet lined with parchment paper.
    - Bake in the preheated oven for 25-30 minutes, or until the pastry is golden brown and the internal temperature of the beef reaches 125°F (52°C) for medium-rare. Adjust baking time for desired doneness.
    - Let the Beef Wellington rest for 10 minutes before slicing.
5. **Serve:**
    - Slice and serve your Beef Wellington with your favorite sides or sauces, such as a red wine reduction or a creamy horseradish sauce.

Tips:

- For a more even cooking, use a meat thermometer to check the internal temperature.
- You can make the duxelles and sear the beef ahead of time; just make sure to let everything cool before wrapping in pastry.

Enjoy the elegance and flavor of this classic Beef Wellington at your next special occasion or holiday meal!

Lemon Herb Roasted Chicken

Ingredients:

For the Chicken:

- 1 whole chicken (about 4-5 pounds), patted dry
- 1 large lemon, halved
- 4 cloves garlic, smashed
- 1 bunch fresh thyme (or 1 tablespoon dried thyme)
- 1 bunch fresh rosemary (or 1 tablespoon dried rosemary)
- 1 bunch fresh parsley (or 1 tablespoon dried parsley)
- 1/4 cup olive oil
- Salt and freshly ground black pepper, to taste

For Roasting:

- 1 large onion, cut into wedges
- 2 carrots, cut into chunks
- 2 celery stalks, cut into chunks
- 1 cup chicken broth or water (for the roasting pan)

Instructions:

1. **Preheat Oven:**
    - Preheat your oven to 425°F (220°C).
2. **Prepare the Chicken:**
    - Remove any giblets or excess fat from the chicken cavity.
    - Pat the chicken dry with paper towels. This helps to ensure a crispy skin.
3. **Season the Chicken:**
    - Rub the inside of the chicken cavity with salt and pepper.
    - Stuff the cavity with lemon halves, garlic cloves, and a few sprigs of thyme, rosemary, and parsley.
    - Rub the outside of the chicken with olive oil, and season generously with salt and pepper.
    - Rub the remaining thyme, rosemary, and parsley all over the chicken.
4. **Prepare the Roasting Pan:**
    - Place the onion, carrots, and celery in the bottom of a roasting pan. This will create a flavorful base for the chicken and help keep it elevated.
5. **Roast the Chicken:**
    - Place the chicken, breast-side up, on top of the vegetables in the roasting pan.
    - Pour the chicken broth or water into the bottom of the pan. This helps to keep the chicken moist and creates a flavorful base for gravy or sauce.
6. **Roast and Baste:**

- Roast the chicken in the preheated oven for about 1 ¼ to 1 ½ hours, or until the internal temperature of the chicken reaches 165°F (74°C) in the thickest part of the thigh.
- Baste the chicken with the pan juices every 20-30 minutes for a golden, crispy skin. If the skin starts to get too dark, you can cover the chicken loosely with aluminum foil.

7. **Rest the Chicken:**
   - Once the chicken is cooked through, remove it from the oven and transfer it to a cutting board. Let it rest for 15 minutes before carving. This allows the juices to redistribute throughout the meat.
8. **Serve:**
   - Carve the chicken and serve with the roasted vegetables and any additional side dishes you like. You can also use the pan drippings to make a simple gravy if desired.

Tips:

- For extra flavor, you can also add a splash of white wine to the roasting pan.
- If you have fresh herbs, feel free to mix and match according to your preference. Fresh herbs usually provide a more intense flavor.

Enjoy your Lemon Herb Roasted Chicken with a side of roasted potatoes, a crisp salad, or your favorite vegetables for a complete and satisfying meal!

Creamy Tomato Basil Soup

Ingredients:

- 2 tablespoons olive oil
- 1 medium onion, finely chopped
- 3 cloves garlic, minced
- 2 (14.5-ounce) cans diced tomatoes (or 4 cups fresh tomatoes, peeled and chopped)
- 1 cup tomato sauce
- 1 cup vegetable or chicken broth
- 1 teaspoon sugar (optional, to taste)
- 1 teaspoon dried basil (or 1 tablespoon fresh basil, chopped)
- ½ teaspoon dried oregano
- Salt and freshly ground black pepper, to taste
- ½ cup heavy cream or half-and-half
- ¼ cup fresh basil leaves, chopped (for garnish)

Instructions:

1. **Sauté the Aromatics:**
    - In a large pot, heat olive oil over medium heat.
    - Add the chopped onion and cook until softened and translucent, about 5-7 minutes.
    - Add the minced garlic and cook for an additional 1-2 minutes until fragrant.
2. **Add Tomatoes and Broth:**
    - Stir in the diced tomatoes, tomato sauce, and vegetable or chicken broth.
    - Add the sugar (if using), dried basil, oregano, salt, and pepper.
    - Bring the mixture to a simmer. Reduce heat and let it cook for about 15-20 minutes to allow the flavors to meld.
3. **Blend the Soup:**
    - Using an immersion blender, blend the soup directly in the pot until smooth. Alternatively, you can carefully transfer the soup in batches to a blender and blend until smooth. (Be cautious with hot liquids.)
4. **Add Cream:**
    - Return the blended soup to the pot (if using a regular blender) and stir in the heavy cream or half-and-half.
    - Simmer the soup for an additional 5 minutes, but do not bring it to a boil.
5. **Adjust Seasoning:**
    - Taste the soup and adjust the seasoning with additional salt, pepper, or sugar as needed.
6. **Serve:**
    - Ladle the soup into bowls and garnish with chopped fresh basil leaves.
    - Serve hot with a side of crusty bread or a grilled cheese sandwich.

Tips:

- **Fresh Tomatoes:** If using fresh tomatoes, you may want to peel them first. Blanching them in boiling water for a minute can make the skins easier to remove.
- **Cream Alternatives:** For a lighter version, you can use whole milk or a non-dairy milk alternative, though this may affect the creaminess.
- **Make Ahead:** This soup can be made ahead of time and stored in the refrigerator for up to 4 days or frozen for up to 3 months. Reheat gently and add a splash of cream if needed when reheating.

This Creamy Tomato Basil Soup is a classic that's both easy to make and incredibly satisfying. Enjoy it as a cozy meal or a delicious starter!

Garlic Parmesan Stuffed Mushrooms

Ingredients:

- 1 pound large button mushrooms or cremini mushrooms
- 2 tablespoons olive oil
- 3 cloves garlic, minced
- ½ cup grated Parmesan cheese
- ¼ cup breadcrumbs (preferably panko for extra crunch)
- 2 tablespoons fresh parsley, chopped (plus extra for garnish)
- 1 tablespoon fresh thyme leaves (or 1 teaspoon dried thyme)
- Salt and freshly ground black pepper, to taste
- 2 tablespoons unsalted butter, melted

Instructions:

1. **Preheat Oven:**
    - Preheat your oven to 375°F (190°C).
2. **Prepare the Mushrooms:**
    - Clean the mushrooms with a damp paper towel to remove any dirt.
    - Gently remove the stems from the mushroom caps and set them aside. (You can finely chop the stems to include in the filling, if desired.)
3. **Make the Filling:**
    - In a medium skillet, heat the olive oil over medium heat.
    - Add the minced garlic and cook for about 1 minute, or until fragrant (be careful not to burn the garlic).
    - If using, add the chopped mushroom stems and cook for an additional 2-3 minutes until softened.
    - In a bowl, combine the cooked garlic (and mushroom stems if using), grated Parmesan cheese, breadcrumbs, chopped parsley, and thyme.
    - Season the mixture with salt and freshly ground black pepper to taste.
    - Stir in the melted butter until the filling is well combined and slightly moist.
4. **Stuff the Mushrooms:**
    - Using a small spoon, fill each mushroom cap generously with the garlic Parmesan filling, pressing it down slightly to pack it in.
5. **Bake:**
    - Arrange the stuffed mushrooms on a baking sheet or in a baking dish.
    - Bake in the preheated oven for 15-20 minutes, or until the mushrooms are tender and the tops are golden brown.
6. **Garnish and Serve:**
    - Remove the mushrooms from the oven and garnish with additional chopped parsley if desired.
    - Serve warm or at room temperature.

Tips:

- **Cheese Variations:** You can substitute the Parmesan cheese with other hard cheeses like Asiago or Pecorino Romano for a different flavor profile.
- **Make Ahead:** These mushrooms can be assembled ahead of time and refrigerated until ready to bake. Just add a few extra minutes to the baking time if they are cold from the fridge.
- **For Extra Crunch:** Mix some additional breadcrumbs with a little melted butter and sprinkle on top of the mushrooms before baking.

Garlic Parmesan Stuffed Mushrooms are a crowd-pleasing appetizer with a rich, savory flavor that pairs perfectly with a variety of dishes. Enjoy them at your next gathering or as a delicious snack!

Spinach Artichoke Dip with Crostini

Ingredients:

For the Dip:

- 1 tablespoon olive oil
- 1 small onion, finely chopped
- 2 cloves garlic, minced
- 1 (10-ounce) package frozen chopped spinach, thawed and squeezed dry
- 1 (14-ounce) can artichoke hearts, drained and chopped
- 1 cup sour cream
- ½ cup mayonnaise
- 1 cup grated Parmesan cheese
- 1 cup shredded mozzarella cheese
- ½ teaspoon dried thyme
- ½ teaspoon dried basil
- Salt and freshly ground black pepper, to taste
- Optional: ¼ teaspoon red pepper flakes (for a bit of heat)

For the Crostini:

- 1 baguette, sliced into ¼-inch rounds
- 2 tablespoons olive oil
- 1 garlic clove, peeled and halved (for rubbing on crostini)

Instructions:

1. **Preheat Oven:**
   - Preheat your oven to 375°F (190°C).
2. **Prepare the Dip:**
   - Heat the olive oil in a large skillet over medium heat.
   - Add the chopped onion and cook until softened and translucent, about 5 minutes.
   - Add the minced garlic and cook for an additional 1 minute, until fragrant.
   - In a large bowl, combine the cooked onions and garlic with the thawed spinach, chopped artichokes, sour cream, mayonnaise, Parmesan cheese, mozzarella cheese, thyme, basil, salt, and pepper. Stir until well combined.
   - Transfer the mixture to a baking dish (about 8x8 inches) and smooth the top.
3. **Bake the Dip:**
   - Bake in the preheated oven for 25-30 minutes, or until the dip is hot and bubbly, and the top is golden brown.
4. **Prepare the Crostini:**
   - While the dip is baking, prepare the crostini.
   - Arrange the baguette slices on a baking sheet.
   - Brush both sides of the baguette slices with olive oil.

- Toast in the oven for about 5-7 minutes, flipping halfway through, until golden and crispy. You can do this at the same time as baking the dip, just keep an eye on the crostini to avoid burning.
- Once toasted, rub each crostini with the cut side of the garlic clove for a hint of garlic flavor.

5. **Serve:**
    - Remove the dip from the oven and let it cool slightly before serving.
    - Serve the warm dip with the toasted crostini on the side for dipping.

Tips:

- **Creaminess:** For an extra creamy dip, you can add a little bit of cream cheese or substitute part of the sour cream with Greek yogurt.
- **Make Ahead:** You can prepare the dip in advance and refrigerate it. When ready to serve, bake it as directed. The crostini can also be made ahead and stored in an airtight container.
- **Add-Ins:** Feel free to add other ingredients like chopped sun-dried tomatoes, cooked bacon, or different cheeses to customize the dip to your taste.

Enjoy your Spinach Artichoke Dip with Crostini—it's a classic appetizer that's sure to be a hit at any gathering!

Chicken Marsala

Ingredients:

For the Chicken:

- 4 boneless, skinless chicken breasts
- Salt and freshly ground black pepper, to taste
- 1 cup all-purpose flour (for dredging)
- 3 tablespoons olive oil
- 3 tablespoons unsalted butter

For the Marsala Sauce:

- 1 cup Marsala wine (use dry Marsala for a less sweet sauce)
- 1 cup chicken broth
- 1 cup sliced mushrooms (cremini, button, or a mix)
- 2 cloves garlic, minced
- 1 tablespoon fresh parsley, chopped (for garnish)
- 1 tablespoon cornstarch mixed with 2 tablespoons water (optional, for thickening)
- Salt and freshly ground black pepper, to taste

Instructions:

1. **Prepare the Chicken:**
   - Place the chicken breasts between two sheets of plastic wrap or parchment paper. Gently pound them to an even thickness, about ½ inch thick, using a meat mallet or rolling pin. This helps them cook evenly.
   - Season both sides of the chicken breasts with salt and pepper.
   - Dredge each chicken breast in flour, shaking off the excess.
2. **Cook the Chicken:**
   - In a large skillet, heat olive oil and 1 tablespoon of butter over medium-high heat.
   - Add the chicken breasts and cook for about 4-5 minutes on each side, or until golden brown and cooked through. The internal temperature should reach 165°F (74°C). Remove the chicken from the skillet and set aside on a plate. Cover loosely with foil to keep warm.
3. **Make the Sauce:**
   - In the same skillet, add the remaining 2 tablespoons of butter. Once melted, add the sliced mushrooms and cook until they start to brown and become tender, about 5 minutes.
   - Add the minced garlic and cook for another 1 minute, or until fragrant.
   - Pour in the Marsala wine and scrape up any browned bits from the bottom of the skillet.
   - Bring the wine to a simmer and let it reduce by half, about 3-4 minutes.
   - Add the chicken broth and continue to simmer for another 5 minutes.

- If you prefer a thicker sauce, mix the cornstarch and water in a small bowl to make a slurry. Stir the slurry into the sauce and simmer until thickened.
4. **Finish the Dish:**
    - Return the chicken breasts to the skillet, spooning the sauce and mushrooms over them. Simmer for an additional 2-3 minutes to heat the chicken through and let the flavors meld.
    - Adjust the seasoning with salt and pepper as needed.
5. **Serve:**
    - Garnish with chopped fresh parsley.
    - Serve the Chicken Marsala over pasta, mashed potatoes, or with a side of vegetables to soak up the delicious sauce.

Tips:

- **Marsala Wine:** If you can't find Marsala wine, you can use a combination of dry white wine and a splash of brandy as a substitute, but it won't be quite the same.
- **Mushrooms:** For extra flavor, you can use a mix of different mushrooms like shiitake, oyster, or portobello.
- **Make Ahead:** You can prepare the chicken and sauce in advance and reheat gently before serving. The flavors often improve after a day.

Chicken Marsala is a flavorful and elegant dish that's perfect for a weeknight dinner or special occasion. Enjoy!

Stuffed Bell Peppers

Ingredients:

- 4 large bell peppers (any color)
- 1 pound ground beef (or ground turkey, chicken, or a vegetarian substitute)
- 1 small onion, finely chopped
- 2 cloves garlic, minced
- 1 cup cooked rice (white, brown, or any preferred variety)
- 1 (14.5-ounce) can diced tomatoes (or 1 cup fresh tomatoes, chopped)
- 1 cup shredded cheese (cheddar, mozzarella, or your choice)
- 2 tablespoons tomato paste
- 1 teaspoon dried oregano
- 1 teaspoon dried basil
- Salt and freshly ground black pepper, to taste
- 1 tablespoon olive oil (for cooking)
- Fresh parsley or basil, chopped (for garnish, optional)

Instructions:

1. **Preheat Oven:**
   - Preheat your oven to 375°F (190°C).
2. **Prepare the Bell Peppers:**
   - Cut the tops off the bell peppers and remove the seeds and membranes.
   - If needed, trim the bottom of the peppers slightly so they stand upright in the baking dish. Be careful not to cut through.
3. **Cook the Filling:**
   - In a large skillet, heat olive oil over medium heat.
   - Add the chopped onion and cook until softened, about 5 minutes.
   - Add the minced garlic and cook for an additional 1 minute, until fragrant.
   - Add the ground beef to the skillet. Cook until browned and cooked through, breaking it up with a spoon as it cooks. Drain any excess fat if necessary.
   - Stir in the tomato paste, diced tomatoes, cooked rice, dried oregano, dried basil, salt, and pepper. Cook for another 5 minutes, allowing the flavors to meld.
   - Remove from heat and stir in ½ cup of the shredded cheese.
4. **Stuff the Peppers:**
   - Spoon the filling into each bell pepper, packing it down slightly. Place the stuffed peppers in a baking dish.
5. **Bake:**
   - Sprinkle the remaining ½ cup of shredded cheese on top of each stuffed pepper.
   - Cover the baking dish with aluminum foil and bake in the preheated oven for 30 minutes.
   - Remove the foil and bake for an additional 10-15 minutes, or until the peppers are tender and the cheese is melted and bubbly.
6. **Serve:**

- Remove from the oven and let cool slightly before serving.
- Garnish with chopped fresh parsley or basil if desired.

Tips:

- **Variations:** You can add other vegetables to the filling, such as corn, black beans, or mushrooms, or use different types of cheese.
- **Rice:** For a quicker option, you can use pre-cooked rice or even quinoa as a substitute.
- **Make Ahead:** Stuffed peppers can be assembled ahead of time and stored in the refrigerator for up to 24 hours before baking. You may need to add a few extra minutes to the baking time if baking from cold.

Stuffed Bell Peppers are a hearty and satisfying dish that's easy to customize and perfect for a family meal. Enjoy!

Baked Ziti with Italian Sausage

Ingredients:

- 1 pound ziti pasta
- 1 pound Italian sausage (sweet or hot, based on preference), casings removed
- 1 small onion, finely chopped
- 3 cloves garlic, minced
- 1 (28-ounce) can crushed tomatoes
- 1 (15-ounce) can tomato sauce
- 1 (6-ounce) can tomato paste
- 1 cup water (or red wine for a richer flavor)
- 2 teaspoons dried basil
- 1 teaspoon dried oregano
- 1 teaspoon sugar (optional, to balance acidity)
- Salt and freshly ground black pepper, to taste
- 1/2 cup chopped fresh parsley (plus extra for garnish)
- 2 cups shredded mozzarella cheese
- 1 cup grated Parmesan cheese
- 1 cup ricotta cheese (optional, for extra creaminess)

Instructions:

1. **Preheat Oven:**
   - Preheat your oven to 375°F (190°C).
2. **Cook the Pasta:**
   - Bring a large pot of salted water to a boil. Add the ziti pasta and cook until just al dente, according to package instructions. Drain and set aside.
3. **Prepare the Meat Sauce:**
   - In a large skillet or saucepan, cook the Italian sausage over medium heat until browned and fully cooked, breaking it up with a spoon as it cooks. Remove the cooked sausage with a slotted spoon and set aside, leaving the fat in the pan.
   - Add the chopped onion to the skillet and cook until softened, about 5 minutes. Add the minced garlic and cook for another minute, until fragrant.
   - Stir in the crushed tomatoes, tomato sauce, tomato paste, and water (or red wine). Mix well.
   - Return the cooked sausage to the pan. Add dried basil, dried oregano, sugar (if using), salt, and pepper. Simmer the sauce for about 15 minutes to allow the flavors to meld.
   - Stir in the chopped parsley and remove from heat.
4. **Combine Pasta and Sauce:**
   - In a large bowl, mix the cooked ziti with about 2 cups of the meat sauce.
   - If using, gently fold in the ricotta cheese for extra creaminess.
5. **Assemble the Dish:**
   - Spread a thin layer of meat sauce on the bottom of a 9x13-inch baking dish.

- Add half of the ziti mixture, spreading it evenly in the dish.
- Top with 1 cup of shredded mozzarella cheese.
- Add another layer of meat sauce over the mozzarella cheese.
- Top with the remaining ziti mixture and spread evenly.
- Pour the remaining meat sauce over the top.
- Sprinkle with the remaining mozzarella cheese and grated Parmesan cheese.

6. **Bake:**
   - Cover the baking dish with aluminum foil and bake in the preheated oven for 25 minutes.
   - Remove the foil and bake for an additional 10-15 minutes, or until the top is golden and bubbly.
7. **Serve:**
   - Let the baked ziti cool for a few minutes before serving.
   - Garnish with additional chopped parsley if desired.

Tips:

- **Make Ahead:** You can assemble the baked ziti ahead of time and refrigerate it for up to 24 hours before baking. Add a few extra minutes to the baking time if baking from cold.
- **Freezing:** Baked ziti freezes well. To freeze, assemble the dish, cover tightly with foil, and freeze. When ready to bake, thaw in the refrigerator overnight and bake as directed.
- **Cheese Options:** You can customize the cheese blend to include other favorites like provolone or fontina for a different flavor.

Enjoy your Baked Ziti with Italian Sausage—a classic comfort food that's sure to be a hit at your next meal!

Seafood Paella

Ingredients:

- **For the Base:**
    - 2 tablespoons olive oil
    - 1 onion, finely chopped
    - 1 red bell pepper, diced
    - 4 cloves garlic, minced
    - 1 (14.5-ounce) can diced tomatoes (or 1 cup fresh tomatoes, chopped)
    - 1 cup frozen peas (thawed)
    - 1 teaspoon smoked paprika
    - 1 teaspoon ground cumin
    - 1/2 teaspoon saffron threads (optional, for authentic flavor and color)
    - 1/2 teaspoon dried thyme
    - Salt and freshly ground black pepper, to taste
- **For the Rice:**
    - 2 cups short-grain or paella rice (such as Bomba or Arborio)
    - 4 cups chicken or seafood broth
    - 1/2 cup dry white wine (optional)
- **For the Seafood:**
    - 1/2 pound large shrimp, peeled and deveined
    - 1/2 pound mussels or clams, scrubbed and debearded
    - 1/2 pound squid or calamari, sliced into rings
    - 1 cup frozen or fresh small seafood (such as peas or small scallops)
- **For Garnish:**
    - 1 lemon, cut into wedges
    - Fresh parsley, chopped

Instructions:

1. **Prepare the Paella Base:**
    - Heat the olive oil in a large paella pan or wide, shallow skillet over medium heat.
    - Add the chopped onion and cook until softened, about 5 minutes.
    - Add the diced red bell pepper and cook for another 3-4 minutes.
    - Stir in the minced garlic and cook for 1 minute until fragrant.
    - Add the diced tomatoes, smoked paprika, ground cumin, saffron threads (if using), dried thyme, salt, and pepper. Cook for about 5 minutes, allowing the tomatoes to break down and the spices to bloom.
2. **Cook the Rice:**
    - Stir in the rice and cook for 2 minutes, allowing it to toast slightly and absorb the flavors.
    - Pour in the chicken or seafood broth and white wine (if using). Bring to a simmer.

- Reduce the heat to low, cover the pan with a lid or foil, and cook for about 15-20 minutes, or until the rice is tender and has absorbed most of the liquid. Avoid stirring the rice during this time to allow the socarrat (crusty bottom) to form.

3. **Add the Seafood:**
   - Gently stir in the shrimp, mussels (or clams), squid, and small seafood (if using). Arrange them evenly over the top of the rice.
   - Cover the pan again and cook for an additional 5-7 minutes, or until the seafood is cooked through and the mussels (or clams) have opened. Discard any mussels or clams that do not open.

4. **Finish and Serve:**
   - Remove the pan from the heat and let it rest for 5 minutes. This helps the flavors meld and allows the rice to finish cooking.
   - Garnish with lemon wedges and chopped fresh parsley.
   - Serve directly from the pan, allowing everyone to scoop out their portion.

Tips:

- **Saffron:** For an authentic paella flavor and beautiful color, saffron is traditional but optional. If unavailable, you can use a pinch of turmeric as a substitute.
- **Rice:** Short-grain rice is crucial for paella as it absorbs flavors well and creates a creamy texture.
- **Seafood Variations:** Feel free to customize the seafood based on availability or preference. Lobster, crab, or other shellfish can also be great additions.
- **Socarrat:** The crispy, caramelized bottom layer of rice (socarrat) is a prized feature of paella. Avoid stirring the rice after adding the broth to help develop this crust.

Seafood Paella is a festive and flavorful dish that's perfect for sharing with family and friends. Enjoy the taste of Spain right at home!

Vegetable Lasagna

Ingredients:

For the Lasagna:

- 12 lasagna noodles (regular or no-boil)
- 2 tablespoons olive oil
- 1 medium onion, chopped
- 3 cloves garlic, minced
- 1 medium zucchini, sliced
- 1 medium yellow squash, sliced
- 1 red bell pepper, diced
- 1 cup mushrooms, sliced
- 1 cup baby spinach or kale, chopped
- 2 cups ricotta cheese
- 1 large egg
- 1 cup shredded mozzarella cheese
- ½ cup grated Parmesan cheese
- 3 cups marinara sauce (store-bought or homemade)
- 1 tablespoon dried basil
- 1 teaspoon dried oregano
- Salt and freshly ground black pepper, to taste
- Fresh basil or parsley, chopped (for garnish, optional)

Instructions:

1. **Preheat Oven:**
   - Preheat your oven to 375°F (190°C).
2. **Cook the Lasagna Noodles:**
   - If using regular lasagna noodles, cook them according to the package instructions until al dente. Drain and lay them out on a lightly oiled sheet of parchment paper to prevent sticking. If using no-boil noodles, skip this step.
3. **Prepare the Vegetables:**
   - Heat olive oil in a large skillet over medium heat.
   - Add the chopped onion and cook until softened, about 5 minutes.
   - Add the minced garlic and cook for 1 minute until fragrant.
   - Add the zucchini, yellow squash, red bell pepper, and mushrooms. Cook until the vegetables are tender, about 7-10 minutes.
   - Stir in the chopped spinach or kale and cook until wilted. Season with dried basil, dried oregano, salt, and pepper. Remove from heat and set aside.
4. **Prepare the Cheese Mixture:**
   - In a medium bowl, combine the ricotta cheese with the egg, ½ cup of the shredded mozzarella cheese, and ¼ cup of the grated Parmesan cheese. Mix well and set aside.

5. **Assemble the Lasagna:**
    - Spread a thin layer of marinara sauce on the bottom of a 9x13-inch baking dish.
    - Place a layer of lasagna noodles on top of the sauce.
    - Spread one-third of the ricotta cheese mixture over the noodles.
    - Add one-third of the vegetable mixture on top of the ricotta.
    - Spoon a layer of marinara sauce over the vegetables.
    - Repeat the layering process two more times, finishing with a layer of marinara sauce.
    - Sprinkle the remaining 1 cup of shredded mozzarella cheese and ¼ cup of grated Parmesan cheese on top.
6. **Bake:**
    - Cover the baking dish with aluminum foil (to prevent the cheese from burning) and bake in the preheated oven for 30 minutes.
    - Remove the foil and bake for an additional 10-15 minutes, or until the cheese is melted and bubbly, and the lasagna is heated through.
7. **Cool and Serve:**
    - Let the lasagna cool for about 10 minutes before slicing. This helps it set and makes it easier to serve.
    - Garnish with chopped fresh basil or parsley if desired.

Tips:

- **Make Ahead:** You can assemble the lasagna in advance and refrigerate it for up to 24 hours before baking. Add a few extra minutes to the baking time if baking from cold.
- **Freeze:** To freeze, assemble the lasagna and cover tightly with foil. Freeze for up to 3 months. Thaw overnight in the refrigerator before baking. Add extra baking time if needed.
- **Cheese Variations:** You can add other cheeses like fontina, provolone, or goat cheese to the ricotta mixture for a different flavor.

Vegetable Lasagna is a comforting and satisfying dish that's perfect for a family dinner or for feeding a crowd. Enjoy the layers of flavor and the creamy, cheesy goodness!

Pulled Pork Sliders

Ingredients:

For the Pulled Pork:

- 4-5 pounds pork shoulder (also called pork butt)
- 2 tablespoons olive oil
- 1 large onion, chopped
- 4 cloves garlic, minced
- 1 cup barbecue sauce (store-bought or homemade)
- 1 cup chicken broth or water
- 2 tablespoons apple cider vinegar
- 2 tablespoons brown sugar
- 1 tablespoon smoked paprika
- 1 tablespoon chili powder
- 1 teaspoon ground cumin
- 1 teaspoon dried oregano
- Salt and freshly ground black pepper, to taste

For the Sliders:

- 12-16 slider buns or small hamburger buns
- Coleslaw (optional, for topping)
- Pickles (optional, for topping)
- Extra barbecue sauce (for serving)

Instructions:

1. **Prepare the Pork Shoulder:**
    - Pat the pork shoulder dry with paper towels and season it generously with salt and pepper. You can also apply a dry rub of smoked paprika, chili powder, ground cumin, and dried oregano if desired.
2. **Sear the Pork (Optional but recommended):**
    - Heat olive oil in a large skillet or Dutch oven over medium-high heat.
    - Sear the pork shoulder on all sides until browned, about 4-5 minutes per side. This step adds extra flavor but can be skipped if you're short on time.
3. **Cook the Pork:**
    - Transfer the seared pork shoulder to a slow cooker or Instant Pot.
    - In the same skillet, add chopped onions and cook until softened, about 5 minutes. Add minced garlic and cook for 1 minute more.
    - Stir in barbecue sauce, chicken broth (or water), apple cider vinegar, and brown sugar. Mix well.
    - Pour the sauce mixture over the pork shoulder in the slow cooker or Instant Pot.
4. **Slow Cooker Method:**

- Cover and cook on low for 8-10 hours, or on high for 4-5 hours, until the pork is very tender and easily shreds with a fork.
5. **Instant Pot Method:**
    - Cover and cook on high pressure for 60 minutes. Allow the pressure to release naturally for 10 minutes before doing a quick release.
6. **Shred the Pork:**
    - Remove the pork shoulder from the cooker and transfer it to a large bowl. Use two forks to shred the meat. If you prefer, you can also use your hands.
    - Return the shredded pork to the cooking liquid and stir well to coat.
7. **Assemble the Sliders:**
    - Split the slider buns and toast them lightly, if desired.
    - Spoon the pulled pork onto the bottom half of each bun.
    - Top with coleslaw and pickles if using.
    - Drizzle with extra barbecue sauce if desired.
    - Place the top half of the bun on top to complete the slider.
8. **Serve:**
    - Arrange the sliders on a platter and serve warm.

Tips:

- **Make Ahead:** Pulled pork can be made in advance and refrigerated for up to 3 days or frozen for up to 3 months. Reheat gently before serving.
- **Variations:** Customize the flavor of the pulled pork by using different barbecue sauces or adding spices to the rub. You can also use a pork loin or tenderloin if you prefer a leaner option.
- **Toppings:** Experiment with different toppings like sautéed onions, jalapeños, or cheese.

Pulled Pork Sliders are a crowd-pleaser that combines tender, flavorful pork with the convenience of slider buns. Enjoy these delicious sliders at your next gathering!

Pesto Pasta Salad

Ingredients:

- **For the Pasta Salad:**
    - 12 ounces pasta (such as rotini, penne, or farfalle)
    - 1 cup cherry or grape tomatoes, halved
    - 1 cup fresh mozzarella balls (or cubed mozzarella)
    - 1/2 cup black olives, sliced (optional)
    - 1/2 cup red bell pepper, diced
    - 1/4 cup red onion, finely chopped
    - 1/4 cup pine nuts or toasted walnuts (optional, for added crunch)
    - Fresh basil leaves, for garnish (optional)
- **For the Pesto:**
    - 2 cups fresh basil leaves
    - 1/2 cup pine nuts or walnuts
    - 1/2 cup grated Parmesan cheese
    - 2 cloves garlic
    - 1/2 cup extra-virgin olive oil
    - Juice of 1 lemon
    - Salt and freshly ground black pepper, to taste

Instructions:

1. **Cook the Pasta:**
    - Bring a large pot of salted water to a boil.
    - Add the pasta and cook according to the package instructions until al dente.
    - Drain the pasta and rinse under cold water to stop the cooking process and cool the pasta quickly. Drain well and transfer to a large mixing bowl.
2. **Prepare the Pesto:**
    - In a food processor or blender, combine the basil leaves, pine nuts (or walnuts), grated Parmesan cheese, and garlic. Pulse until finely chopped.
    - With the processor running, slowly drizzle in the olive oil until the mixture is smooth and creamy.
    - Add lemon juice, salt, and pepper to taste. Blend again to combine. Adjust seasoning if necessary.
3. **Combine Salad Ingredients:**
    - Add the pesto to the cooled pasta and toss until evenly coated.
    - Gently fold in the cherry tomatoes, mozzarella balls, black olives (if using), red bell pepper, and red onion.
    - Sprinkle in the pine nuts or toasted walnuts if desired, and give the salad one final toss.
4. **Chill and Serve:**
    - Cover the pasta salad and refrigerate for at least 30 minutes to allow the flavors to meld.

- Before serving, give the salad a good stir and garnish with fresh basil leaves if desired.

Tips:

- **Pasta Choice:** You can use any pasta shape you prefer or have on hand. Just ensure it's cooked al dente to hold up well in the salad.
- **Vegetables:** Feel free to add other vegetables like cucumbers, roasted red peppers, or artichoke hearts based on your preference or what you have available.
- **Make Ahead:** This pasta salad can be made a day in advance and stored in the refrigerator. It may need a bit more pesto or olive oil before serving, as the pasta can absorb the dressing.

Pesto Pasta Salad is a versatile and flavorful dish that's sure to be a hit at any gathering. Enjoy the fresh, herby goodness of this delicious salad!

Mushroom Risotto

Ingredients:

- **For the Risotto:**
    - 1/2 cup dry white wine (optional)
    - 4 cups chicken or vegetable broth
    - 2 tablespoons olive oil
    - 1 small onion, finely chopped
    - 2 cloves garlic, minced
    - 1 pound mushrooms (such as cremini, button, or a mix), cleaned and sliced
    - 1 1/2 cups Arborio or Carnaroli rice
    - 1/2 cup grated Parmesan cheese
    - 2 tablespoons unsalted butter
    - Salt and freshly ground black pepper, to taste
    - Fresh parsley or chives, chopped (for garnish, optional)

Instructions:

1. **Prepare the Broth:**
    - In a medium saucepan, heat the chicken or vegetable broth over low heat. Keep warm throughout the cooking process.
2. **Cook the Mushrooms:**
    - In a large skillet or saucepan, heat 1 tablespoon of olive oil over medium heat.
    - Add the sliced mushrooms and cook until they release their moisture and become golden brown, about 8-10 minutes. Season with salt and pepper to taste.
    - Remove the mushrooms from the skillet and set aside.
3. **Start the Risotto:**
    - In a large, heavy-bottomed pot or Dutch oven, heat the remaining 1 tablespoon of olive oil over medium heat.
    - Add the chopped onion and cook until softened, about 5 minutes.
    - Add the minced garlic and cook for 1 minute, until fragrant.
4. **Add the Rice:**
    - Stir in the Arborio or Carnaroli rice and cook for 1-2 minutes, until the rice is lightly toasted and coated with the oil and onion mixture.
5. **Deglaze with Wine (Optional):**
    - Pour in the white wine and stir until it has mostly evaporated.
6. **Cook the Risotto:**
    - Begin adding the warm broth to the rice one ladleful at a time, stirring constantly and allowing each addition to be absorbed before adding more.
    - Continue adding the broth and stirring for about 18-20 minutes, or until the rice is creamy and cooked al dente. You may not need all of the broth, or you might need a bit more, so adjust as needed.
7. **Finish the Risotto:**
    - Stir the cooked mushrooms back into the risotto.

- Remove from heat and stir in the butter and grated Parmesan cheese until melted and well combined.
- Adjust seasoning with salt and pepper to taste.
8. **Serve:**
    - Spoon the risotto onto serving plates or bowls.
    - Garnish with fresh parsley or chives if desired.

Tips:

- **Constant Stirring:** Stirring the risotto frequently helps release the rice's natural starches, which gives the risotto its creamy texture.
- **Broth Temperature:** Keep the broth warm but not boiling to ensure it is absorbed properly by the rice.
- **Rice Choice:** Arborio or Carnaroli rice are the best choices for risotto due to their high starch content, which contributes to the creaminess.

Mushroom Risotto is a rich and satisfying dish that showcases the earthy flavor of mushrooms and the creamy texture of well-cooked risotto. Enjoy this comforting meal!

Quiche Lorraine

Ingredients:

For the Pie Crust:

- 1 1/4 cups all-purpose flour
- 1/4 teaspoon salt
- 1/2 cup (1 stick) unsalted butter, chilled and cut into small pieces
- 1/4 cup ice water (more if needed)

For the Filling:

- 6 slices bacon, chopped
- 1/2 cup onion, finely chopped
- 1 cup shredded Gruyère cheese (or Swiss cheese)
- 3 large eggs
- 1 1/2 cups heavy cream
- 1/2 cup whole milk
- 1/4 teaspoon ground nutmeg
- 1/4 teaspoon black pepper
- Salt, to taste
- Fresh chives or parsley, chopped (for garnish, optional)

Instructions:

1. **Prepare the Pie Crust:**
   - In a medium bowl, mix the flour and salt.
   - Cut in the chilled butter using a pastry cutter or your fingers until the mixture resembles coarse crumbs.
   - Gradually add ice water, stirring until the dough comes together. You might need a bit more water if the dough is too dry.
   - Form the dough into a disc, wrap it in plastic wrap, and refrigerate for at least 30 minutes.
2. **Preheat Oven:**
   - Preheat your oven to 375°F (190°C).
3. **Prepare the Crust:**
   - On a floured surface, roll out the dough to fit a 9-inch pie dish or tart pan. Carefully transfer the dough to the pan, pressing it into the bottom and up the sides. Trim any excess dough.
   - Prick the bottom of the crust with a fork to prevent bubbling.
4. **Pre-Bake the Crust:**
   - Line the crust with parchment paper or aluminum foil and fill it with pie weights or dried beans.
   - Bake in the preheated oven for 15 minutes.

- Remove the parchment and weights, and bake for an additional 5 minutes, until the crust is lightly golden. Remove from the oven and set aside.

5. **Prepare the Filling:**
    - In a skillet over medium heat, cook the chopped bacon until crispy. Remove with a slotted spoon and drain on paper towels.
    - In the same skillet, add the chopped onion and cook until softened, about 5 minutes. Set aside.
    - In a large bowl, whisk together the eggs, heavy cream, milk, nutmeg, black pepper, and a pinch of salt.

6. **Assemble the Quiche:**
    - Spread the cooked bacon and onion evenly over the pre-baked crust.
    - Sprinkle the shredded cheese on top.
    - Pour the egg mixture over the bacon, onion, and cheese.

7. **Bake:**
    - Bake in the preheated oven for 35-40 minutes, or until the filling is set and the top is golden brown. A knife inserted into the center should come out clean.

8. **Cool and Serve:**
    - Allow the quiche to cool slightly before slicing. Garnish with chopped chives or parsley if desired.

Tips:

- **Crust:** If you prefer a flakier crust, consider using a food processor to blend the dough quickly.
- **Variations:** You can add other ingredients like sautéed mushrooms, spinach, or sun-dried tomatoes to customize the quiche.
- **Storage:** Quiche Lorraine can be made ahead of time and stored in the refrigerator for up to 3 days. It can also be frozen for up to 1 month. Reheat gently in the oven.

Quiche Lorraine is a versatile and delicious dish that's always a crowd-pleaser. Enjoy it warm or at room temperature!

Buffalo Chicken Wings

Ingredients:

For the Chicken Wings:

- 2 pounds chicken wings (drumettes and flats)
- 1 tablespoon vegetable oil
- 1 teaspoon garlic powder
- 1 teaspoon onion powder
- 1 teaspoon paprika
- 1/2 teaspoon salt
- 1/2 teaspoon black pepper

For the Buffalo Sauce:

- 1/2 cup hot sauce (such as Frank's RedHot)
- 1/4 cup unsalted butter
- 1 tablespoon white vinegar
- 1/4 teaspoon garlic powder
- 1/4 teaspoon onion powder
- 1/4 teaspoon cayenne pepper (optional, for extra heat)
- Salt, to taste

For Serving:

- Celery sticks
- Carrot sticks
- Ranch or blue cheese dressing

Instructions:

1. **Prepare the Chicken Wings:**
   - If not pre-cut, separate the chicken wings into drumettes and flats by cutting through the joint with a sharp knife. Discard the wing tips or save them for making stock.
   - In a large bowl, toss the wings with vegetable oil, garlic powder, onion powder, paprika, salt, and black pepper until evenly coated.
2. **Cook the Wings:**
   - **For Baking:**
     - Preheat your oven to 425°F (220°C).
     - Line a baking sheet with parchment paper or lightly grease it. Place a wire rack on top of the baking sheet.
     - Arrange the wings in a single layer on the wire rack.
     - Bake for 40-45 minutes, flipping halfway through, until the wings are crispy and golden brown.

- **For Frying:**
  - Heat vegetable oil in a deep fryer or large pot to 350°F (175°C).
  - Fry the wings in batches for about 8-10 minutes, or until they are golden brown and crispy. Remove with a slotted spoon and drain on paper towels.
- **For Air Frying:**
  - Preheat the air fryer to 360°F (180°C).
  - Arrange the wings in a single layer in the air fryer basket. Cook for 25-30 minutes, shaking the basket halfway through.

3. **Make the Buffalo Sauce:**
   - While the wings are cooking, combine the hot sauce, butter, white vinegar, garlic powder, onion powder, and cayenne pepper (if using) in a saucepan over medium heat.
   - Stir until the butter is melted and the sauce is smooth. Adjust salt to taste.
4. **Toss the Wings:**
   - Once the wings are cooked, place them in a large bowl.
   - Pour the Buffalo sauce over the wings and toss until they are well coated.
5. **Serve:**
   - Transfer the wings to a serving platter.
   - Serve with celery sticks, carrot sticks, and your choice of ranch or blue cheese dressing.

Tips:

- **Crispier Wings:** For even crispier wings, pat them dry with paper towels before seasoning and baking or frying.
- **Adjusting Spice Level:** Adjust the amount of hot sauce and cayenne pepper to suit your taste if you prefer a milder or spicier sauce.
- **Resting Time:** Let the wings rest for a few minutes after cooking to allow the skin to firm up.

Buffalo Chicken Wings are always a hit with their tangy, spicy flavor and crispy texture. Enjoy them with your favorite dipping sauces and sides!

Beef Stroganoff

Ingredients:

- **For the Beef Stroganoff:**
    - 1 pound beef sirloin or tenderloin, cut into thin strips
    - 2 tablespoons vegetable oil or unsalted butter
    - 1 medium onion, finely chopped
    - 2 cloves garlic, minced
    - 8 ounces mushrooms, sliced (cremini, button, or a mix)
    - 1 tablespoon all-purpose flour
    - 1 cup beef broth
    - 1 cup sour cream (full-fat for best results)
    - 2 tablespoons Dijon mustard
    - 1 tablespoon Worcestershire sauce
    - 1 teaspoon paprika
    - Salt and freshly ground black pepper, to taste
    - Fresh parsley, chopped (for garnish)
- **For Serving:**
    - Cooked egg noodles, rice, or mashed potatoes

Instructions:

1. **Prepare the Beef:**
    - Season the beef strips with salt and pepper.
    - Heat the vegetable oil or butter in a large skillet over medium-high heat.
2. **Brown the Beef:**
    - Add the beef strips to the skillet in a single layer. Avoid overcrowding the pan to ensure even browning.
    - Cook the beef for 2-3 minutes per side until browned but not fully cooked through. Remove the beef from the skillet and set aside.
3. **Cook the Vegetables:**
    - In the same skillet, add a bit more oil or butter if needed. Add the chopped onion and cook until softened, about 5 minutes.
    - Add the minced garlic and cook for 1 minute, until fragrant.
    - Add the sliced mushrooms and cook until they release their moisture and are golden brown, about 5-7 minutes.
4. **Make the Sauce:**
    - Sprinkle the flour over the mushrooms and onions, stirring to combine. Cook for 1-2 minutes to eliminate the raw flour taste.
    - Gradually add the beef broth, stirring constantly to avoid lumps. Bring the mixture to a simmer and cook for about 5 minutes, until the sauce has thickened slightly.
5. **Add the Beef Back:**
    - Return the browned beef to the skillet.

- Stir in the sour cream, Dijon mustard, Worcestershire sauce, and paprika. Mix until well combined.
- Simmer for 5-7 minutes, or until the beef is cooked through and the sauce is creamy. Adjust seasoning with salt and pepper to taste.

6. **Serve:**
   - Spoon the Beef Stroganoff over cooked egg noodles, rice, or mashed potatoes.
   - Garnish with chopped fresh parsley if desired.

Tips:

- **Beef Selection:** Use tender cuts of beef like sirloin or tenderloin for the best results. Avoid tougher cuts that require longer cooking times.
- **Sour Cream:** For a richer flavor, use full-fat sour cream. You can substitute Greek yogurt if desired.
- **Thickening the Sauce:** If you prefer a thicker sauce, you can simmer it longer to reduce it further or mix a bit of cornstarch with water and add it to the sauce.

Beef Stroganoff is a comforting and delicious dish that's perfect for a cozy meal. Enjoy the creamy, savory flavors with your favorite side!

Thai Green Curry

Ingredients:

For the Green Curry Paste:

- 1 tablespoon vegetable oil
- 2-3 tablespoons Thai green curry paste (store-bought or homemade)
- 1 tablespoon chopped fresh cilantro stems (optional, for extra flavor)
- 1 teaspoon chopped galangal or ginger (optional, for added depth)
- 2-3 Thai bird's eye chilies, chopped (optional, for extra heat)

For the Curry:

- 1 can (14 oz) coconut milk
- 1 cup chicken or vegetable broth
- 2 tablespoons fish sauce (or soy sauce for a vegetarian option)
- 1 tablespoon palm sugar or brown sugar
- 1-2 tablespoons lime juice
- 1 cup bamboo shoots (canned or fresh), sliced (optional)
- 1 cup baby corn, halved
- 1 bell pepper, sliced
- 1 cup snow peas or green beans
- 1 cup Thai eggplant or regular eggplant, cut into bite-sized pieces
- 1 pound chicken breast or thighs, sliced (or tofu for a vegetarian option)
- Fresh basil leaves (preferably Thai basil) for garnish
- Fresh cilantro leaves for garnish (optional)
- Cooked jasmine rice for serving

Instructions:

1. **Prepare the Curry Paste:**
    - Heat vegetable oil in a large skillet or wok over medium heat.
    - Add the Thai green curry paste and cook, stirring constantly, until fragrant, about 1-2 minutes. If using, add chopped cilantro stems, galangal or ginger, and bird's eye chilies during this step.
2. **Cook the Curry:**
    - Add the coconut milk to the skillet and stir to combine with the curry paste. Bring to a gentle simmer.
    - Add the chicken or vegetable broth, fish sauce, and palm sugar. Stir until the sugar is dissolved.
    - Add the sliced chicken or tofu and cook until nearly cooked through, about 5-7 minutes.
3. **Add the Vegetables:**

- Add the bamboo shoots, baby corn, bell pepper, snow peas or green beans, and eggplant.
- Simmer until the vegetables are tender and the chicken is cooked through, about 10-15 minutes.
4. **Finish the Curry:**
    - Stir in the lime juice. Taste and adjust seasoning if needed, adding more fish sauce, sugar, or lime juice to balance the flavors.
    - If the curry is too thick, you can add a bit more broth or coconut milk to reach your desired consistency.
5. **Serve:**
    - Serve the Thai Green Curry hot, garnished with fresh basil and cilantro leaves.
    - Accompany with cooked jasmine rice.

Tips:

- **Green Curry Paste:** Thai green curry paste is available in most grocery stores or Asian markets. You can also make your own paste using ingredients like green chilies, garlic, lemongrass, and spices.
- **Protein Choice:** Feel free to use other proteins like shrimp or beef, or add more vegetables for a vegetarian version.
- **Adjusting Heat:** Adjust the amount of green curry paste to control the heat level of the curry. Start with a smaller amount and taste as you go.
- **Thai Eggplant:** If you can't find Thai eggplant, regular eggplant works fine. Just make sure to cut it into bite-sized pieces.

Thai Green Curry is a wonderfully versatile and flavorful dish that brings a taste of Thailand to your kitchen. Enjoy the rich, spicy, and creamy curry with your favorite accompaniments!

Eggplant Parmesan

Ingredients:

For the Eggplant:

- 2 large eggplants
- Salt (for draining the eggplant)
- 1 cup all-purpose flour
- 2 large eggs
- 1 cup breadcrumbs (preferably Italian-style)
- 1/2 cup grated Parmesan cheese
- 1/2 teaspoon dried oregano
- 1/2 teaspoon dried basil
- Vegetable oil (for frying)

For the Marinara Sauce:

- 2 cups marinara sauce (store-bought or homemade)
- 1 clove garlic, minced
- 1 tablespoon olive oil
- 1/2 teaspoon dried basil
- 1/2 teaspoon dried oregano
- Salt and freshly ground black pepper, to taste

For Assembling:

- 1 1/2 cups shredded mozzarella cheese
- 1/2 cup grated Parmesan cheese
- Fresh basil leaves, for garnish (optional)

Instructions:

1. **Prepare the Eggplant:**
    - Slice the eggplants into 1/4-inch thick rounds.
    - Lay the slices in a single layer on a baking sheet or a colander. Sprinkle both sides generously with salt. This helps to draw out excess moisture and bitterness.
    - Let the eggplant slices sit for about 30 minutes. Rinse off the salt and pat the slices dry with paper towels.
2. **Bread the Eggplant:**
    - Set up a breading station with three shallow dishes:
        - In the first dish, place the flour.
        - In the second dish, beat the eggs.
        - In the third dish, mix the breadcrumbs with 1/2 cup grated Parmesan cheese, dried oregano, and dried basil.

- Dip each eggplant slice first into the flour, then into the beaten eggs, and finally coat with the breadcrumb mixture, pressing gently to adhere.
3. **Fry the Eggplant:**
    - Heat about 1/4 inch of vegetable oil in a large skillet over medium heat.
    - Fry the eggplant slices in batches until golden brown and crispy, about 2-3 minutes per side. Add more oil as needed between batches.
    - Transfer the fried eggplant slices to a paper towel-lined plate to drain excess oil.
4. **Prepare the Marinara Sauce:**
    - In a medium saucepan, heat olive oil over medium heat.
    - Add the minced garlic and cook until fragrant, about 1 minute.
    - Stir in the marinara sauce, dried basil, dried oregano, salt, and pepper. Simmer for 10-15 minutes to blend the flavors.
5. **Assemble the Eggplant Parmesan:**
    - Preheat your oven to 375°F (190°C).
    - Spread a thin layer of marinara sauce on the bottom of a baking dish (9x13-inch or similar).
    - Arrange a layer of fried eggplant slices over the sauce.
    - Spread a layer of marinara sauce over the eggplant and sprinkle with shredded mozzarella cheese.
    - Repeat the layers (eggplant, marinara sauce, mozzarella) until you have used all the eggplant, ending with a layer of marinara sauce and a generous topping of mozzarella and the remaining 1/2 cup of grated Parmesan cheese.
6. **Bake:**
    - Cover the baking dish with aluminum foil and bake in the preheated oven for 25 minutes.
    - Remove the foil and bake for an additional 10-15 minutes, or until the cheese is bubbly and golden brown.
7. **Garnish and Serve:**
    - Let the Eggplant Parmesan cool for a few minutes before serving.
    - Garnish with fresh basil leaves if desired.

Tips:

- **Eggplant Preparation:** Salting the eggplant helps remove excess moisture and bitterness. Make sure to rinse and dry the slices thoroughly.
- **Baking Option:** For a lighter version, you can bake the breaded eggplant slices instead of frying them. Preheat the oven to 400°F (200°C) and bake the slices on a parchment-lined baking sheet for 20-25 minutes, flipping halfway through.
- **Homemade Marinara:** Use a homemade marinara sauce for a richer flavor. You can find a simple recipe or use your favorite store-bought sauce.

Eggplant Parmesan is a comforting and satisfying dish that's sure to please anyone who loves Italian cuisine. Enjoy the layers of crispy eggplant, tangy marinara, and melted cheese!

Grilled Salmon with Avocado Salsa

Ingredients:

For the Salmon:

- 4 salmon fillets (6 oz each), skin-on or skinless
- 2 tablespoons olive oil
- 1 tablespoon lemon juice
- 1 teaspoon garlic powder
- 1 teaspoon paprika
- 1/2 teaspoon dried oregano
- Salt and freshly ground black pepper, to taste

For the Avocado Salsa:

- 2 ripe avocados, diced
- 1 cup cherry tomatoes, halved
- 1/4 cup red onion, finely chopped
- 1/4 cup fresh cilantro, chopped
- 1 jalapeño, seeded and finely chopped (optional, for heat)
- 1 tablespoon lime juice
- Salt and freshly ground black pepper, to taste

For Serving:

- Lemon wedges
- Fresh cilantro or parsley, for garnish (optional)

Instructions:

1. **Prepare the Salmon:**
    - Preheat your grill to medium-high heat.
    - In a small bowl, mix together olive oil, lemon juice, garlic powder, paprika, dried oregano, salt, and pepper.
    - Brush the salmon fillets with the olive oil mixture on both sides.
2. **Grill the Salmon:**
    - Place the salmon fillets on the grill, skin-side down if the skin is on.
    - Grill the salmon for 4-6 minutes per side, depending on the thickness of the fillets. The salmon should be opaque and flake easily with a fork. Avoid overcooking to keep the salmon moist and tender.
    - Remove the salmon from the grill and let it rest for a few minutes.
3. **Make the Avocado Salsa:**
    - In a medium bowl, gently combine the diced avocados, cherry tomatoes, red onion, cilantro, and jalapeño (if using).

-
  -
    - Add lime juice and season with salt and pepper to taste. Gently toss to combine. Be careful not to mash the avocados; you want to keep the salsa chunky.
  4. **Serve:**
     - Place the grilled salmon fillets on serving plates.
     - Top each fillet with a generous portion of avocado salsa.
     - Garnish with lemon wedges and additional fresh cilantro or parsley if desired.

Tips:

- **Grilling Salmon:** To prevent the salmon from sticking to the grill, ensure the grill grates are well-oiled. You can also use a grill basket or foil if needed.
- **Avocado Salsa:** Prepare the salsa just before serving to keep the avocados fresh and green. If you need to prepare it ahead of time, add the lime juice just before serving to prevent browning.
- **Flavor Variations:** You can add other ingredients to the salsa like diced cucumber or corn for extra texture and flavor.

Grilled Salmon with Avocado Salsa is a light, nutritious, and flavorful meal that's easy to prepare and perfect for any occasion. Enjoy the combination of tender, smoky salmon with the bright and creamy avocado salsa!

Chicken Fajitas

Ingredients:

For the Marinade:

- 1/4 cup olive oil
- Juice of 1 lime
- 2 cloves garlic, minced
- 1 teaspoon ground cumin
- 1 teaspoon smoked paprika
- 1 teaspoon chili powder
- 1/2 teaspoon ground coriander
- 1/2 teaspoon onion powder
- 1/2 teaspoon garlic powder
- 1/4 teaspoon cayenne pepper (optional, for extra heat)
- Salt and freshly ground black pepper, to taste

For the Fajitas:

- 1 1/2 pounds boneless, skinless chicken breasts or thighs, sliced into thin strips
- 2 tablespoons olive oil
- 1 large onion, sliced
- 1 red bell pepper, sliced
- 1 green bell pepper, sliced
- 1 yellow bell pepper, sliced

For Serving:

- Flour or corn tortillas
- Shredded lettuce
- Sliced tomatoes
- Sliced avocado or guacamole
- Sour cream
- Shredded cheese (cheddar or Mexican blend)
- Salsa or pico de gallo
- Lime wedges
- Fresh cilantro, chopped (optional)

Instructions:

1. **Marinate the Chicken:**
    - In a bowl, whisk together olive oil, lime juice, minced garlic, cumin, smoked paprika, chili powder, ground coriander, onion powder, garlic powder, cayenne pepper (if using), salt, and pepper.

- Add the sliced chicken to the marinade and mix until well coated. Cover and refrigerate for at least 30 minutes, or up to 4 hours for more flavor.

2. **Cook the Chicken:**
   - Heat 2 tablespoons of olive oil in a large skillet or grill pan over medium-high heat.
   - Add the marinated chicken strips to the skillet in a single layer. Cook for 5-7 minutes, stirring occasionally, until the chicken is cooked through and slightly charred. Remove the chicken from the skillet and set aside.

3. **Sauté the Vegetables:**
   - In the same skillet, add a bit more olive oil if needed. Add the sliced onion and bell peppers.
   - Sauté for 5-7 minutes, or until the vegetables are tender and slightly caramelized. Season with a pinch of salt and pepper.

4. **Combine:**
   - Return the cooked chicken to the skillet with the vegetables. Toss everything together to combine and heat through.

5. **Serve:**
   - Warm the tortillas according to the package instructions or in a dry skillet.
   - Serve the chicken and vegetable mixture with the warm tortillas and your choice of toppings.

Tips:

- **Marinating:** Marinating the chicken for at least 30 minutes helps to infuse it with flavor. For best results, marinate overnight.
- **Cooking:** If you prefer a smoky flavor, you can cook the chicken and vegetables on a grill or grill pan.
- **Toppings:** Feel free to customize your toppings based on your preferences. Add things like sliced jalapeños for extra heat or pickled onions for a tangy kick.
- **Vegetables:** You can add other vegetables like mushrooms or zucchini for variety.

Chicken Fajitas are perfect for a casual dinner or a fun gathering. Enjoy the vibrant flavors and customizable toppings with your family and friends!

Lentil Soup with Ham

Ingredients:

- **For the Soup:**
    - 1 tablespoon olive oil
    - 1 large onion, chopped
    - 2 cloves garlic, minced
    - 2 medium carrots, peeled and diced
    - 2 celery stalks, diced
    - 1 cup dried green or brown lentils, rinsed and drained
    - 1 bay leaf
    - 1 teaspoon dried thyme
    - 1/2 teaspoon smoked paprika
    - 1/2 teaspoon ground cumin
    - 1/2 teaspoon black pepper
    - 1/2 teaspoon salt (or to taste)
    - 6 cups chicken or vegetable broth
    - 1 cup diced cooked ham (leftover or pre-cooked)
    - 1 can (14.5 oz) diced tomatoes, with their juice
    - 1 cup chopped kale or spinach (optional)
    - 2 tablespoons fresh parsley, chopped (for garnish)
- **For Serving:**
    - Crusty bread or crackers

Instructions:

1. **Sauté the Vegetables:**
    - Heat olive oil in a large pot or Dutch oven over medium heat.
    - Add the chopped onion and cook until softened and translucent, about 5 minutes.
    - Stir in the minced garlic and cook for an additional 1 minute, until fragrant.
    - Add the diced carrots and celery, and cook for another 5 minutes, stirring occasionally.
2. **Add Lentils and Spices:**
    - Stir in the rinsed lentils, bay leaf, dried thyme, smoked paprika, ground cumin, black pepper, and salt.
    - Cook for 1-2 minutes, allowing the spices to toast slightly and become aromatic.
3. **Add Broth and Tomatoes:**
    - Pour in the chicken or vegetable broth and add the diced tomatoes with their juice.
    - Stir to combine, and bring the mixture to a boil.
4. **Simmer the Soup:**
    - Reduce the heat to low and cover the pot. Simmer for 25-30 minutes, or until the lentils are tender and cooked through.

- Stir occasionally, and add more broth or water if needed to reach your desired consistency.
5. **Add Ham and Greens:**
    - Stir in the diced ham and chopped kale or spinach (if using).
    - Continue to cook for an additional 5-10 minutes, until the ham is heated through and the greens are wilted.
6. **Finish and Serve:**
    - Remove the bay leaf from the soup.
    - Taste and adjust seasoning with additional salt and pepper if needed.
    - Garnish with fresh parsley before serving.
7. **Serve:**
    - Ladle the soup into bowls and serve with crusty bread or crackers.

Tips:

- **Lentils:** Green or brown lentils hold their shape well during cooking, but you can use red lentils if you prefer a softer texture.
- **Ham:** Use leftover ham, ham steak, or even ham hocks for additional flavor. Adjust the salt in the soup based on the saltiness of the ham.
- **Vegetables:** Feel free to add other vegetables like potatoes or bell peppers for extra nutrition and flavor.
- **Thickening:** If you like a thicker soup, you can blend a portion of the soup with an immersion blender or regular blender and then return it to the pot.

Lentil Soup with Ham is a nutritious and satisfying meal that's perfect for chilly days. Enjoy the rich flavors and comforting warmth of this hearty soup!

Crispy Pork Belly Tacos

Ingredients:

For the Pork Belly:

- 1 pound pork belly, skin-on
- 1 tablespoon vegetable oil
- 1 tablespoon sea salt
- 1 teaspoon ground black pepper
- 1 teaspoon smoked paprika
- 1 teaspoon ground cumin
- 1 teaspoon garlic powder
- 1 teaspoon onion powder

For the Taco Toppings:

- 1 cup shredded cabbage (green or purple)
- 1/2 cup fresh cilantro, chopped
- 1 small red onion, finely diced
- 1 avocado, sliced
- 1 lime, cut into wedges
- 1/4 cup sour cream (optional)
- 1 tablespoon hot sauce (optional)

For the Tortillas:

- 8 small corn or flour tortillas

For Garnish (optional):

- Additional fresh cilantro
- Thinly sliced radishes

Instructions:

1. **Prepare the Pork Belly:**
    - Preheat your oven to 300°F (150°C).
    - Score the skin of the pork belly in a crosshatch pattern, being careful not to cut into the meat.
    - Rub the pork belly all over with vegetable oil, then season with sea salt, black pepper, smoked paprika, ground cumin, garlic powder, and onion powder. Ensure the seasoning gets into the scored areas.
    - Place the pork belly on a rack set over a roasting pan, skin-side up. This allows the fat to drain off during cooking and helps the skin get crispy.
2. **Roast the Pork Belly:**

- Roast the pork belly in the preheated oven for 2.5 to 3 hours, or until the meat is tender and the skin is crispy.
- If the skin isn't crispy enough, increase the oven temperature to 425°F (220°C) and roast for an additional 15-20 minutes, or until the skin is bubbly and crispy. Keep an eye on it to avoid burning.

3. **Crisp the Pork Belly (Optional):**
   - For extra crispiness, you can place the pork belly under a broiler for a few minutes, turning occasionally until the skin is golden and crisp. Watch closely to prevent burning.
4. **Rest and Slice the Pork Belly:**
   - Remove the pork belly from the oven and let it rest for about 10 minutes before slicing.
   - Cut the pork belly into small, bite-sized pieces.
5. **Prepare the Toppings:**
   - While the pork belly is resting, prepare your taco toppings. Mix shredded cabbage with chopped cilantro and lime juice if desired.
   - Dice the red onion and slice the avocado.
6. **Warm the Tortillas:**
   - Heat the tortillas in a dry skillet over medium heat or wrap them in foil and warm them in the oven. Alternatively, you can microwave them for a few seconds.
7. **Assemble the Tacos:**
   - Place a few pieces of crispy pork belly on each tortilla.
   - Top with shredded cabbage, diced red onion, and avocado slices.
   - Add a dollop of sour cream if using and drizzle with hot sauce if desired.
   - Squeeze lime wedges over the tacos for extra flavor.
   - Garnish with additional fresh cilantro and thinly sliced radishes if desired.
8. **Serve:**
   - Serve the tacos immediately while they're warm and crispy. Enjoy!

Tips:

- **Pork Belly:** Make sure to pat the pork belly dry before seasoning to help achieve a crispy skin. If you have a meat thermometer, aim for an internal temperature of about 190°F (88°C) for tender meat.
- **Toppings:** Customize your toppings to your taste. Pickled red onions or a fresh salsa could be great additions.
- **Crisping the Skin:** The key to crispy skin is roasting at a lower temperature for a longer time and then finishing with a high temperature or broiling.

Crispy Pork Belly Tacos offer a delightful mix of crunchy and tender textures with fresh, zesty toppings. Enjoy these tacos for a fantastic meal that's sure to impress!

Butternut Squash Soup

Ingredients:

- **For the Soup:**
    - 1 large butternut squash (about 3 pounds), peeled, seeded, and cut into 1-inch cubes
    - 1 tablespoon olive oil
    - 1 large onion, chopped
    - 2 cloves garlic, minced
    - 2 carrots, peeled and chopped
    - 2 celery stalks, chopped
    - 4 cups chicken or vegetable broth
    - 1 cup water (or more broth as needed)
    - 1/2 teaspoon ground cumin
    - 1/2 teaspoon ground nutmeg
    - 1/2 teaspoon ground cinnamon
    - Salt and freshly ground black pepper, to taste
    - 1/2 cup heavy cream or coconut milk (optional, for added creaminess)
    - 1 tablespoon maple syrup or honey (optional, for added sweetness)
- **For Garnish (optional):**
    - Crumbled bacon or crispy chickpeas
    - Fresh parsley or cilantro
    - A drizzle of cream or coconut milk
    - Pumpkin seeds or toasted nuts

Instructions:

1. **Prepare the Butternut Squash:**
    - Preheat your oven to 400°F (200°C).
    - Toss the butternut squash cubes with a little olive oil, salt, and pepper. Spread them out in a single layer on a baking sheet.
    - Roast for 25-30 minutes, or until the squash is tender and caramelized, stirring halfway through.
2. **Cook the Vegetables:**
    - In a large pot or Dutch oven, heat the remaining 1 tablespoon of olive oil over medium heat.
    - Add the chopped onion and cook until softened and translucent, about 5 minutes.
    - Stir in the minced garlic, carrots, and celery, and cook for an additional 5-7 minutes, until the vegetables begin to soften.
3. **Combine Ingredients:**
    - Add the roasted butternut squash to the pot with the sautéed vegetables.
    - Pour in the chicken or vegetable broth and 1 cup of water. Stir in the ground cumin, nutmeg, cinnamon, salt, and pepper.

- Bring the mixture to a simmer and cook for 10-15 minutes, allowing the flavors to meld and the vegetables to become tender.
4. **Blend the Soup:**
    - Use an immersion blender to blend the soup until smooth. If you don't have an immersion blender, you can carefully transfer the soup in batches to a regular blender and blend until smooth. Be cautious with hot liquids.
    - Return the blended soup to the pot if using a regular blender.
5. **Finish the Soup:**
    - Stir in the heavy cream or coconut milk, if using, and adjust seasoning with additional salt, pepper, or maple syrup/honey for added sweetness if desired.
    - Heat the soup gently until warmed through.
6. **Serve:**
    - Ladle the soup into bowls and garnish with your choice of toppings.
    - Serve hot with crusty bread or a side salad.

Tips:

- **Roasting:** Roasting the butternut squash brings out its natural sweetness and adds depth of flavor to the soup. Don't skip this step if you can.
- **Creaminess:** For a lighter version, you can skip the cream or use coconut milk. You can also blend in some cooked potatoes for added creaminess.
- **Spices:** Adjust the spices to your taste. Adding a pinch of cayenne pepper can give the soup a bit of heat if you like a spicier flavor.

Butternut Squash Soup is not only delicious but also packed with nutrients. It's a versatile recipe that can be customized with various spices and garnishes, making it a perfect addition to your meal rotation. Enjoy the comforting and sweet flavors of this delightful soup!

BBQ Chicken Pizza

Ingredients:

For the Pizza Dough:

- 1 1/2 cups warm water (110°F/45°C)
- 2 1/4 teaspoons (1 packet) active dry yeast
- 1 teaspoon sugar
- 3 1/2 to 4 cups all-purpose flour
- 2 tablespoons olive oil
- 1 teaspoon salt

For the BBQ Chicken:

- 2 cups cooked chicken, shredded or diced (grilled, rotisserie, or poached)
- 1/2 cup BBQ sauce (store-bought or homemade)

For the Pizza:

- 1/2 cup BBQ sauce (for drizzling)
- 1 1/2 cups shredded mozzarella cheese
- 1/2 cup red onion, thinly sliced
- 1/2 cup sliced bell peppers (any color)
- 1/4 cup fresh cilantro, chopped (optional, for garnish)

For the Garnish (optional):

- Extra BBQ sauce for drizzling
- Additional fresh cilantro

Instructions:

1. **Prepare the Dough:**
   - In a small bowl, combine warm water, yeast, and sugar. Let it sit for about 5 minutes, or until it becomes frothy.
   - In a large bowl, mix 3 1/2 cups of flour with salt. Create a well in the center and add the yeast mixture and olive oil.
   - Mix until a dough forms. If the dough is too sticky, add additional flour, 1 tablespoon at a time, until it's manageable.
   - Transfer the dough to a floured surface and knead for about 5-7 minutes until smooth and elastic.
   - Place the dough in a lightly oiled bowl, cover with a damp cloth or plastic wrap, and let it rise in a warm place for 1 hour or until doubled in size.
2. **Prepare the BBQ Chicken:**

- In a medium bowl, toss the shredded or diced chicken with 1/2 cup of BBQ sauce until well coated. Set aside.
3. **Preheat the Oven:**
    - Preheat your oven to 475°F (245°C). If you're using a pizza stone, place it in the oven while it heats.
4. **Roll Out the Dough:**
    - Once the dough has risen, punch it down and transfer it to a floured surface. Roll out the dough into a 12-inch round or to fit your pizza pan.
    - Transfer the rolled dough to a lightly floured pizza peel or an oiled pizza pan.
5. **Assemble the Pizza:**
    - Spread 1/2 cup of BBQ sauce evenly over the pizza dough, leaving a small border around the edges.
    - Evenly distribute the BBQ chicken over the sauce.
    - Sprinkle shredded mozzarella cheese over the chicken.
    - Add thinly sliced red onion and bell peppers on top of the cheese.
6. **Bake the Pizza:**
    - Bake the pizza in the preheated oven for 12-15 minutes, or until the crust is golden brown and the cheese is bubbly and slightly browned.
    - If using a pizza stone, transfer the pizza onto the hot stone and bake.
7. **Garnish and Serve:**
    - Remove the pizza from the oven and let it cool for a few minutes.
    - Drizzle additional BBQ sauce over the top if desired.
    - Garnish with fresh cilantro before slicing.
8. **Serve:**
    - Slice the pizza and serve warm.

Tips:

- **Dough Preparation:** You can make the pizza dough ahead of time and refrigerate it for up to 3 days or freeze it for up to 3 months. Let it come to room temperature before using.
- **BBQ Sauce:** Use your favorite BBQ sauce or make your own for a personalized touch. Adjust the sweetness or tanginess according to your taste.
- **Cheese:** Feel free to experiment with different cheeses like cheddar or gouda for a different flavor profile.
- **Vegetables:** You can add other toppings like mushrooms, olives, or jalapeños for extra flavor.

BBQ Chicken Pizza is a delicious and versatile dish that's perfect for a casual dinner or a fun gathering. Enjoy the tangy BBQ flavor combined with melted cheese and tender chicken!

Vegetarian Chili

Ingredients:

- **For the Chili:**
    - 2 tablespoons olive oil
    - 1 large onion, chopped
    - 3 cloves garlic, minced
    - 2 bell peppers (any color), chopped
    - 2 medium carrots, peeled and diced
    - 2 celery stalks, diced
    - 1 zucchini, diced
    - 1 cup corn kernels (fresh, frozen, or canned)
    - 1 can (14.5 oz) diced tomatoes
    - 1 can (6 oz) tomato paste
    - 2 cups vegetable broth
    - 1 can (15 oz) black beans, drained and rinsed
    - 1 can (15 oz) kidney beans, drained and rinsed
    - 1 can (15 oz) chickpeas, drained and rinsed
    - 1 tablespoon chili powder
    - 1 teaspoon ground cumin
    - 1/2 teaspoon smoked paprika
    - 1/2 teaspoon dried oregano
    - 1/4 teaspoon cayenne pepper (optional, for heat)
    - Salt and freshly ground black pepper, to taste
- **For Garnish (optional):**
    - Chopped fresh cilantro
    - Shredded cheese (cheddar or Mexican blend)
    - Sour cream or Greek yogurt
    - Sliced jalapeños
    - Sliced green onions
    - Crushed tortilla chips

Instructions:

1. **Sauté the Vegetables:**
    - Heat olive oil in a large pot or Dutch oven over medium heat.
    - Add the chopped onion and cook until softened and translucent, about 5 minutes.
    - Stir in the minced garlic and cook for an additional 1 minute, until fragrant.
    - Add the chopped bell peppers, carrots, celery, and zucchini. Cook for 5-7 minutes, until the vegetables begin to soften.
2. **Add Tomatoes and Beans:**
    - Stir in the diced tomatoes, tomato paste, and vegetable broth.
    - Add the black beans, kidney beans, chickpeas, and corn kernels. Mix well.
3. **Season the Chili:**

- Add the chili powder, ground cumin, smoked paprika, dried oregano, cayenne pepper (if using), salt, and black pepper.
- Stir to combine and bring the mixture to a simmer.

4. **Simmer the Chili:**
   - Reduce the heat to low and cover the pot. Let the chili simmer for 30-40 minutes, stirring occasionally, until the vegetables are tender and the flavors have melded together.
   - If the chili becomes too thick, add a bit more vegetable broth or water to reach your desired consistency.

5. **Adjust Seasoning:**
   - Taste the chili and adjust seasoning with additional salt, pepper, or spices as needed.

6. **Serve:**
   - Ladle the chili into bowls and garnish with your choice of toppings such as chopped cilantro, shredded cheese, sour cream, sliced jalapeños, sliced green onions, or crushed tortilla chips.

Tips:

- **Beans:** Feel free to use other types of beans, like pinto or navy beans, based on your preference.
- **Spice Level:** Adjust the amount of cayenne pepper and chili powder to control the heat level. You can also add a splash of hot sauce for extra kick.
- **Vegetables:** Customize the chili with other vegetables such as sweet potatoes, butternut squash, or mushrooms for added variety and nutrition.
- **Make Ahead:** Vegetarian chili often tastes even better the next day as the flavors continue to develop. It can be stored in the refrigerator for up to 5 days or frozen for up to 3 months.

Vegetarian Chili is a nutritious, filling meal that's perfect for a family dinner or meal prep. Enjoy the rich, hearty flavors and the versatility of this delicious dish!

Shrimp Scampi

Ingredients:

- **For the Shrimp:**
    - 1 pound large shrimp, peeled and deveined
    - 1 tablespoon olive oil
    - 1 tablespoon unsalted butter
- **For the Scampi Sauce:**
    - 4 cloves garlic, minced
    - 1/4 teaspoon red pepper flakes (optional, for heat)
    - 1/2 cup dry white wine (like Sauvignon Blanc) or chicken broth
    - Juice of 1 lemon
    - 1/4 cup chopped fresh parsley
    - 1/4 cup grated Parmesan cheese (optional, for added flavor)
    - Salt and freshly ground black pepper, to taste
- **For Serving:**
    - 8 ounces pasta (linguine, spaghetti, or fettuccine), cooked according to package instructions
    - Lemon wedges
    - Extra chopped parsley for garnish

Instructions:

1. **Prepare the Shrimp:**
    - Pat the shrimp dry with paper towels. This helps them sear properly.
    - Season the shrimp lightly with salt and pepper.
2. **Cook the Shrimp:**
    - Heat olive oil and 1 tablespoon of butter in a large skillet over medium-high heat.
    - Add the shrimp to the skillet in a single layer. Cook for 1-2 minutes on each side, or until the shrimp are pink and opaque. Remove the shrimp from the skillet and set aside.
3. **Prepare the Scampi Sauce:**
    - In the same skillet, add the minced garlic and red pepper flakes (if using). Sauté for 30 seconds to 1 minute, until the garlic is fragrant but not browned.
    - Pour in the white wine (or chicken broth) and lemon juice. Bring to a simmer and cook for 2-3 minutes, allowing the liquid to reduce slightly.
    - Stir in the remaining 1 tablespoon of butter until melted and incorporated into the sauce.
    - Return the cooked shrimp to the skillet and toss to coat in the sauce. Cook for another 1-2 minutes, until the shrimp are heated through and well-coated with the sauce.
    - Stir in the chopped parsley and adjust seasoning with additional salt and pepper, if needed. If using, sprinkle in the grated Parmesan cheese for added richness.
4. **Combine with Pasta:**

- If serving with pasta, toss the cooked pasta into the skillet with the shrimp and sauce, or serve the shrimp and sauce over the pasta.
5. **Serve:**
    - Serve the Shrimp Scampi hot, garnished with additional chopped parsley and lemon wedges on the side for squeezing over the top.
    - Enjoy with a side of crusty bread to soak up the delicious sauce.

Tips:

- **Pasta:** Use a pasta shape that can hold onto the sauce, like linguine or fettuccine. Cook the pasta al dente according to package instructions.
- **Wine:** The white wine adds depth of flavor, but you can substitute chicken broth if you prefer not to use alcohol.
- **Butter:** For a richer sauce, you can add more butter. If you're looking to cut down on fat, you can use less butter and increase the amount of broth.
- **Garlic:** Be careful not to burn the garlic as it cooks quickly and can turn bitter if overcooked.

Shrimp Scampi is a flavorful and elegant dish that's perfect for a weeknight dinner or a special occasion. Enjoy the succulent shrimp and rich, buttery sauce with your favorite pasta or a side of fresh bread!

Sweet and Sour Meatballs

Ingredients:

For the Meatballs:

- 1 pound ground beef (or a mix of beef and pork)
- 1/2 cup breadcrumbs (plain or Italian)
- 1/4 cup grated Parmesan cheese (optional)
- 1/4 cup finely chopped onion
- 1/4 cup chopped parsley (fresh or dried)
- 1 large egg
- 2 cloves garlic, minced
- 1 teaspoon dried oregano
- 1/2 teaspoon salt
- 1/2 teaspoon black pepper

For the Sweet and Sour Sauce:

- 1/2 cup ketchup
- 1/2 cup pineapple juice (or canned pineapple juice)
- 1/4 cup rice vinegar (or white vinegar)
- 1/4 cup brown sugar (packed)
- 1 tablespoon soy sauce
- 1 tablespoon cornstarch
- 2 tablespoons water

For Garnish (optional):

- Chopped green onions
- Sesame seeds

Instructions:

1. **Prepare the Meatballs:**
    - Preheat your oven to 375°F (190°C).
    - In a large bowl, combine ground beef, breadcrumbs, Parmesan cheese (if using), chopped onion, parsley, egg, minced garlic, oregano, salt, and black pepper. Mix until well combined, but be careful not to overmix.
    - Shape the mixture into 1-inch meatballs and place them on a baking sheet lined with parchment paper or a lightly greased rack.
2. **Bake the Meatballs:**
    - Bake the meatballs in the preheated oven for 20-25 minutes, or until they are cooked through and browned on the outside. The internal temperature should reach 160°F (70°C).
3. **Prepare the Sweet and Sour Sauce:**

- While the meatballs are baking, in a medium saucepan, combine ketchup, pineapple juice, rice vinegar, brown sugar, and soy sauce. Stir to combine and bring the mixture to a simmer over medium heat.
  - In a small bowl, mix cornstarch with 2 tablespoons of water to create a slurry.
  - Stir the cornstarch slurry into the simmering sauce and cook for 2-3 minutes, or until the sauce has thickened.
4. **Combine Meatballs and Sauce:**
   - Once the meatballs are done baking, remove them from the oven and transfer them to the saucepan with the sweet and sour sauce.
   - Stir gently to coat the meatballs with the sauce and heat through for 2-3 minutes.
5. **Serve:**
   - Transfer the meatballs to a serving platter or dish.
   - Garnish with chopped green onions and sesame seeds if desired.
   - Serve the Sweet and Sour Meatballs over steamed rice or as an appetizer with toothpicks.

Tips:

- **Meatballs:** For a different flavor, you can use ground turkey or chicken instead of beef.
- **Sauce:** Adjust the sweetness or tanginess of the sauce to your preference by adding more sugar or vinegar.
- **Cornstarch:** Ensure the cornstarch slurry is well mixed to avoid lumps in the sauce.
- **Make Ahead:** You can prepare the meatballs and sauce ahead of time. Store them separately in the refrigerator and combine them when ready to serve.

Sweet and Sour Meatballs are a crowd-pleaser, ideal for parties, family dinners, or as a tasty appetizer. Enjoy the flavorful combination of sweet, tangy, and savory in every bite!

Chicken Alfredo

Ingredients:

For the Chicken:

- 2 large boneless, skinless chicken breasts
- 2 tablespoons olive oil
- 1 teaspoon garlic powder
- 1 teaspoon onion powder
- 1/2 teaspoon dried Italian seasoning (or dried basil and oregano)
- Salt and freshly ground black pepper, to taste

For the Alfredo Sauce:

- 4 tablespoons unsalted butter
- 3 cloves garlic, minced
- 1 cup heavy cream
- 1 cup grated Parmesan cheese
- 1/2 cup chicken broth (or milk for a lighter sauce)
- 1/4 teaspoon ground nutmeg (optional, for added flavor)
- Salt and freshly ground black pepper, to taste

For the Pasta:

- 8 ounces fettuccine, linguine, or your favorite pasta
- Salt (for the pasta water)

For Garnish (optional):

- Chopped fresh parsley
- Extra grated Parmesan cheese

Instructions:

1. **Prepare the Chicken:**
    - Season the chicken breasts with garlic powder, onion powder, dried Italian seasoning, salt, and black pepper.
    - Heat olive oil in a large skillet over medium-high heat.
    - Add the chicken breasts and cook for 5-7 minutes per side, or until the chicken is cooked through and has an internal temperature of 165°F (74°C). The chicken should be golden brown on the outside.
    - Remove the chicken from the skillet and let it rest for a few minutes before slicing into thin strips or bite-sized pieces.
2. **Cook the Pasta:**
    - While the chicken is cooking, bring a large pot of salted water to a boil.

- Cook the pasta according to the package instructions until al dente. Reserve about 1/2 cup of pasta cooking water, then drain the pasta.
3. **Prepare the Alfredo Sauce:**
   - In the same skillet used for the chicken, melt the butter over medium heat.
   - Add the minced garlic and cook for about 1 minute, until fragrant but not browned.
   - Pour in the heavy cream and bring to a gentle simmer. Cook for 2-3 minutes, stirring occasionally, until the cream begins to thicken.
   - Gradually stir in the grated Parmesan cheese until it is melted and the sauce is smooth.
   - Add chicken broth (or milk) to adjust the consistency of the sauce as needed.
   - Season with salt, black pepper, and ground nutmeg (if using).
4. **Combine Pasta and Sauce:**
   - Add the cooked pasta to the skillet with the Alfredo sauce. Toss to coat the pasta evenly with the sauce. If the sauce is too thick, you can add some of the reserved pasta water to reach your desired consistency.
   - Gently fold in the sliced or diced chicken.
5. **Serve:**
   - Transfer the Chicken Alfredo to serving plates or bowls.
   - Garnish with chopped fresh parsley and extra grated Parmesan cheese if desired.
   - Serve immediately while hot.

Tips:

- **Chicken:** For added flavor, marinate the chicken in olive oil, lemon juice, and herbs before cooking. You can also use pre-cooked rotisserie chicken for a quicker option.
- **Creaminess:** Adjust the richness of the sauce by using more or less heavy cream, or by incorporating additional chicken broth or milk.
- **Cheese:** Freshly grated Parmesan cheese works best for a smooth, creamy sauce. Pre-grated cheese can sometimes result in a grainy texture.
- **Pasta:** Save some of the pasta cooking water to help loosen the sauce if needed and to help it adhere better to the pasta.

Chicken Alfredo is a decadent and satisfying meal that's perfect for a special dinner or a comforting weeknight meal. Enjoy the creamy, cheesy goodness combined with tender chicken and perfectly cooked pasta!

Cobb Salad

Ingredients:

For the Salad:

- 4 cups mixed greens (such as romaine, spinach, or arugula)
- 1 cup cooked chicken breast, diced or sliced (grilled, baked, or rotisserie)
- 4 strips of bacon, cooked until crispy and crumbled
- 1 avocado, diced
- 1 cup cherry tomatoes, halved
- 1/2 cup blue cheese or feta cheese, crumbled
- 3 hard-boiled eggs, peeled and sliced
- 1/4 cup red onion, thinly sliced (optional)
- Salt and freshly ground black pepper, to taste

For the Dressing:

- 1/4 cup red wine vinegar
- 1 tablespoon Dijon mustard
- 1 tablespoon honey (or maple syrup)
- 1/2 cup olive oil
- 1 small garlic clove, minced
- Salt and freshly ground black pepper, to taste

Instructions:

1. **Prepare the Ingredients:**
    - **Cook the Chicken:** If not using pre-cooked chicken, season chicken breasts with salt and pepper and cook them using your preferred method (grilling, baking, or pan-searing) until fully cooked. Let them rest for a few minutes before dicing or slicing.
    - **Cook the Bacon:** Cook the bacon in a skillet over medium heat until crispy. Remove from the skillet, let cool slightly, and crumble into pieces.
    - **Hard-Boil the Eggs:** Place eggs in a pot of cold water and bring to a boil. Once boiling, cover the pot and remove from heat. Let the eggs sit for 12 minutes, then transfer to an ice bath to cool. Peel and slice the eggs.
    - **Prepare Vegetables:** Dice the avocado, halve the cherry tomatoes, and thinly slice the red onion if using.
2. **Make the Dressing:**
    - In a small bowl or jar, whisk together the red wine vinegar, Dijon mustard, honey, minced garlic, salt, and pepper.
    - Gradually whisk in the olive oil until the dressing is well combined and emulsified. Adjust seasoning to taste.
3. **Assemble the Salad:**

- On a large platter or individual plates, arrange the mixed greens as the base.
- Neatly arrange the diced chicken, crumbled bacon, diced avocado, cherry tomatoes, crumbled cheese, and sliced hard-boiled eggs on top of the greens.
- Optionally, sprinkle the sliced red onion over the top.
4. **Serve:**
    - Drizzle the dressing over the salad just before serving, or serve the dressing on the side so everyone can add their own.
    - Season with additional salt and pepper if desired.

Tips:

- **Protein:** You can substitute or add other proteins like grilled shrimp or turkey if preferred.
- **Cheese:** Blue cheese is traditional for Cobb Salad, but feta cheese works well too if you prefer a milder flavor.
- **Avocado:** To prevent the avocado from browning, add it just before serving.
- **Dressing:** You can make the dressing ahead of time and store it in the refrigerator for up to a week. Shake or whisk well before using.

Cobb Salad is a versatile and satisfying dish that's perfect for a light lunch or a substantial dinner. It's packed with flavors and textures, making it a favorite for many. Enjoy the freshness and richness of this classic salad!

Stuffed Acorn Squash

Ingredients:

For the Squash:

- 2 medium acorn squashes
- 2 tablespoons olive oil
- Salt and freshly ground black pepper

For the Stuffing:

- 1/2 cup quinoa, rinsed (or use rice, farro, or couscous as a substitute)
- 1 cup vegetable or chicken broth (or water)
- 1 tablespoon olive oil
- 1 small onion, finely chopped
- 2 cloves garlic, minced
- 1 cup diced mushrooms (button, cremini, or shiitake)
- 1/2 cup diced celery
- 1/2 cup diced carrots
- 1/4 cup dried cranberries or raisins
- 1/4 cup chopped nuts (such as pecans, walnuts, or almonds)
- 1/4 cup crumbled feta cheese or shredded mozzarella (optional)
- 1 teaspoon dried thyme or rosemary (or a combination)
- 1/2 teaspoon ground cumin (optional)
- 1/4 teaspoon paprika
- Salt and freshly ground black pepper, to taste
- Fresh parsley or sage for garnish (optional)

Instructions:

1. **Prepare the Acorn Squash:**
    - Preheat your oven to 400°F (200°C).
    - Cut the acorn squashes in half from stem to base. Scoop out the seeds and stringy bits using a spoon.
    - Brush the cut sides of the squash with olive oil and season with salt and pepper.
    - Place the squash cut side down on a baking sheet lined with parchment paper or aluminum foil.
    - Roast in the preheated oven for 25-30 minutes, or until the squash is tender and easily pierced with a fork. The cooking time may vary depending on the size of the squash.
2. **Prepare the Stuffing:**
    - While the squash is roasting, prepare the quinoa according to the package instructions, using vegetable or chicken broth for added flavor.
    - In a large skillet, heat 1 tablespoon of olive oil over medium heat.

- Add the chopped onion and cook for 3-4 minutes, until softened.
- Stir in the minced garlic and cook for an additional 1 minute, until fragrant.
- Add the diced mushrooms, celery, and carrots. Cook for 5-7 minutes, until the vegetables are tender.
- Stir in the dried cranberries (or raisins), chopped nuts, and cooked quinoa. Mix well.
- Season with dried thyme or rosemary, ground cumin (if using), paprika, salt, and pepper. Adjust seasoning to taste.
- Remove from heat and fold in the crumbled feta cheese or shredded mozzarella, if using.

3. **Stuff the Squash:**
    - Once the squash is tender, remove it from the oven and carefully flip it over so the cut side is facing up.
    - Spoon the prepared stuffing into each acorn squash half, packing it in slightly.
4. **Bake the Stuffed Squash:**
    - Return the stuffed squash to the oven and bake for an additional 10-15 minutes, or until the stuffing is heated through and slightly golden on top.
5. **Serve:**
    - Garnish with fresh parsley or sage if desired.
    - Serve hot as a main dish or a side dish.

Tips:

- **Vegetarian Option:** For a vegetarian stuffing, you can use vegetable broth and skip the cheese or use a vegetarian cheese alternative.
- **Add Protein:** For added protein, you can include cooked chicken, sausage, or tofu in the stuffing.
- **Make Ahead:** The stuffing can be prepared ahead of time and stored in the refrigerator. Stuff the squash and bake just before serving.
- **Customization:** Feel free to customize the stuffing with your favorite vegetables, grains, or herbs.

Stuffed Acorn Squash is a nutritious and visually appealing dish that makes a great centerpiece for fall or holiday meals. Enjoy the combination of tender squash and flavorful stuffing!

Beef Tacos with Salsa Verde

Ingredients:

For the Beef Filling:

- 1 pound ground beef
- 1 tablespoon olive oil
- 1 small onion, finely chopped
- 2 cloves garlic, minced
- 1 tablespoon chili powder
- 1 teaspoon ground cumin
- 1 teaspoon smoked paprika
- 1/2 teaspoon dried oregano
- 1/4 teaspoon cayenne pepper (optional, for heat)
- 1/2 cup beef broth (or water)
- Salt and freshly ground black pepper, to taste

For the Salsa Verde:

- 1 pound tomatillos, husked and rinsed
- 2-3 jalapeño peppers (or more, depending on desired heat), stems removed
- 1 small onion, quartered
- 2 cloves garlic, peeled
- 1/2 cup fresh cilantro leaves
- Juice of 1 lime
- Salt and freshly ground black pepper, to taste

For the Tacos:

- 8-10 small tortillas (corn or flour, as preferred)
- 1 cup shredded lettuce
- 1 cup diced tomatoes
- 1/2 cup crumbled queso fresco or shredded cheese
- 1/4 cup chopped fresh cilantro (for garnish)
- Lime wedges (for serving)
- Sour cream or Greek yogurt (optional)

Instructions:

1. **Prepare the Salsa Verde:**
    - Preheat your broiler or grill to high heat.
    - Place the tomatillos, jalapeño peppers, onion, and garlic on a baking sheet.
    - Broil or grill the vegetables for about 5-7 minutes, turning occasionally, until they are charred and softened.
    - Transfer the vegetables to a blender or food processor.

- Add the fresh cilantro leaves and lime juice.
- Blend until smooth. Season with salt and pepper to taste.
- Set aside.
2. **Prepare the Beef Filling:**
    - Heat olive oil in a large skillet over medium heat.
    - Add the chopped onion and cook for 3-4 minutes, until softened.
    - Stir in the minced garlic and cook for 1 minute.
    - Add the ground beef to the skillet. Cook, breaking it up with a spoon, until browned and cooked through, about 5-7 minutes.
    - Drain excess fat if needed.
    - Stir in the chili powder, ground cumin, smoked paprika, dried oregano, and cayenne pepper (if using).
    - Pour in the beef broth and simmer for 5 minutes, allowing the flavors to meld and the liquid to reduce slightly.
    - Season with salt and pepper to taste.
3. **Assemble the Tacos:**
    - Warm the tortillas in a dry skillet or in the oven until pliable.
    - Spoon the seasoned beef filling onto the tortillas.
    - Top with shredded lettuce, diced tomatoes, and crumbled queso fresco or shredded cheese.
    - Drizzle with the prepared salsa verde.
    - Garnish with chopped fresh cilantro.
4. **Serve:**
    - Serve the tacos with lime wedges on the side for squeezing over the top.
    - Optional: Add a dollop of sour cream or Greek yogurt if desired.

Tips:

- **Salsa Verde:** You can make the salsa verde ahead of time and store it in the refrigerator for up to a week. It also freezes well.
- **Beef:** If you prefer, you can use ground turkey, chicken, or beef alternatives. Adjust seasoning accordingly.
- **Toppings:** Customize your tacos with additional toppings such as sliced radishes, avocado, or pickled onions.
- **Tortillas:** For added flavor, try warming the tortillas with a little oil for a crispy edge.

These Beef Tacos with Salsa Verde are packed with flavor and make for a fantastic meal that's both satisfying and fresh. Enjoy the vibrant combination of seasoned beef and tangy salsa verde!

Greek Salad with Lemon Vinaigrette

Ingredients:

For the Salad:

- 3 cups mixed salad greens (such as romaine, arugula, or baby spinach)
- 1 cup cherry tomatoes, halved
- 1 cucumber, peeled and sliced or diced
- 1/2 red onion, thinly sliced
- 1/2 cup Kalamata olives or black olives, pitted
- 1/2 cup crumbled feta cheese
- 1/4 cup sliced radishes (optional)
- 1/4 cup diced bell pepper (any color, optional)

For the Lemon Vinaigrette:

- 1/4 cup freshly squeezed lemon juice (about 1-2 lemons)
- 1/4 cup extra virgin olive oil
- 1 teaspoon Dijon mustard
- 1 small garlic clove, minced
- 1/2 teaspoon dried oregano
- 1/4 teaspoon honey or maple syrup (optional, for a touch of sweetness)
- Salt and freshly ground black pepper, to taste

Instructions:

1. **Prepare the Salad:**
   - In a large salad bowl, combine the mixed greens, cherry tomatoes, cucumber, red onion, olives, and any optional ingredients like radishes and bell peppers.
   - Toss gently to mix the vegetables.
2. **Make the Lemon Vinaigrette:**
   - In a small bowl or jar, whisk together the lemon juice, extra virgin olive oil, Dijon mustard, minced garlic, dried oregano, and honey or maple syrup (if using).
   - Season with salt and freshly ground black pepper to taste.
   - Whisk until the dressing is well combined and emulsified.
3. **Assemble the Salad:**
   - Drizzle the lemon vinaigrette over the salad just before serving.
   - Toss gently to coat the salad with the dressing.
   - Sprinkle crumbled feta cheese on top of the salad.
4. **Serve:**
   - Serve immediately as a fresh, light meal or side dish.

Tips:

- **Veggies:** Feel free to add other traditional Greek salad ingredients like sliced Kalamata olives, capers, or even cooked chickpeas for extra protein.
- **Dressing:** You can make the lemon vinaigrette ahead of time and store it in the refrigerator for up to a week. Shake or whisk well before using.
- **Cheese:** For a different flavor, you can substitute feta with crumbled goat cheese or shredded Parmesan.
- **Greens:** Use a mix of greens or just one type based on your preference for a more customized salad.

Greek Salad with Lemon Vinaigrette is a bright and flavorful dish that highlights the freshness of its ingredients. The tangy vinaigrette pairs perfectly with the crisp vegetables and creamy feta, making it a crowd-pleaser for any occasion. Enjoy!

Salmon Cakes

Ingredients:

For the Salmon Cakes:

- 1 can (14.75 ounces) of pink or red salmon, drained and flaked (or 1 1/2 cups cooked, flaked salmon)
- 1/2 cup breadcrumbs (plain or panko)
- 1/4 cup finely chopped onion
- 1/4 cup finely chopped celery
- 1/4 cup chopped fresh parsley (or 1 tablespoon dried parsley)
- 1 large egg, beaten
- 2 tablespoons mayonnaise
- 1 teaspoon Dijon mustard
- 1 teaspoon lemon juice
- 1/2 teaspoon dried dill (optional)
- 1/2 teaspoon garlic powder
- Salt and freshly ground black pepper, to taste
- 2 tablespoons olive oil or vegetable oil (for frying)

For Serving (optional):

- Lemon wedges
- Tartar sauce or aioli
- Mixed greens or a simple salad

Instructions:

1. **Prepare the Salmon Mixture:**
    - In a large bowl, combine the flaked salmon, breadcrumbs, chopped onion, chopped celery, and chopped parsley.
    - In a separate small bowl, mix together the beaten egg, mayonnaise, Dijon mustard, lemon juice, dried dill (if using), garlic powder, salt, and pepper.
    - Add the egg mixture to the salmon mixture and gently combine until everything is well mixed. Be careful not to overwork the mixture to keep the cakes tender.
2. **Form the Salmon Cakes:**
    - Divide the mixture into 6-8 portions and shape each portion into a patty about 1/2 inch thick.
    - Place the formed patties on a plate or baking sheet.
3. **Cook the Salmon Cakes:**
    - Heat olive oil or vegetable oil in a large skillet over medium heat.
    - Add the salmon cakes to the skillet, being careful not to overcrowd them. Cook for 3-4 minutes per side, or until they are golden brown and crispy on the outside and cooked through on the inside. You may need to cook them in batches.

- Transfer the cooked salmon cakes to a plate lined with paper towels to drain any excess oil.
4. **Serve:**
    - Serve the salmon cakes hot with lemon wedges and tartar sauce or aioli on the side.
    - They can also be served over mixed greens or with a simple salad for a complete meal.

Tips:

- **Salmon:** If using fresh salmon, cook it thoroughly before flaking it. You can also use leftover cooked salmon.
- **Breadcrumbs:** Panko breadcrumbs will give the cakes a crispier texture, but regular breadcrumbs work fine too.
- **Binding:** If the mixture seems too wet and won't hold together well, add a bit more breadcrumbs. If too dry, add a little more mayonnaise or a splash of milk.
- **Baking Option:** For a healthier version, you can bake the salmon cakes. Preheat your oven to 400°F (200°C), place the patties on a baking sheet lined with parchment paper, and bake for 15-20 minutes, flipping halfway through.

Salmon Cakes are not only delicious but also a great way to enjoy the benefits of salmon in a different and tasty form. Enjoy these crispy, flavorful cakes with your favorite sides or sauces!

Roasted Beet and Goat Cheese Salad

Ingredients:

For the Salad:

- 4 medium beets, scrubbed and trimmed
- 2 tablespoons olive oil
- Salt and freshly ground black pepper, to taste
- 4 cups mixed greens (such as arugula, spinach, or baby kale)
- 4 ounces goat cheese, crumbled
- 1/4 cup chopped walnuts or pecans (toasted if preferred)
- 1/4 cup dried cranberries or pomegranate seeds (optional)
- 1/4 cup thinly sliced red onion (optional)

For the Vinaigrette:

- 1/4 cup balsamic vinegar
- 2 tablespoons extra virgin olive oil
- 1 teaspoon Dijon mustard
- 1 teaspoon honey or maple syrup (optional, for sweetness)
- 1 small garlic clove, minced
- Salt and freshly ground black pepper, to taste

Instructions:

1. **Roast the Beets:**
   - Preheat your oven to 400°F (200°C).
   - Wrap each beet individually in aluminum foil and place them on a baking sheet.
   - Roast the beets in the preheated oven for about 45-60 minutes, or until they are tender and easily pierced with a fork. The cooking time will depend on the size of the beets.
   - Remove the beets from the oven and let them cool slightly.
   - Once cool enough to handle, peel the skins off the beets. The skins should slip off easily. Cut the beets into bite-sized wedges or cubes.
2. **Prepare the Vinaigrette:**
   - In a small bowl or jar, whisk together the balsamic vinegar, extra virgin olive oil, Dijon mustard, honey or maple syrup (if using), minced garlic, salt, and pepper.
   - Taste and adjust seasoning if necessary.
3. **Assemble the Salad:**
   - In a large salad bowl, place the mixed greens.
   - Top with the roasted beet pieces.
   - Sprinkle the crumbled goat cheese over the top.
   - Add the toasted nuts, dried cranberries or pomegranate seeds, and red onion if using.

- Drizzle the vinaigrette over the salad just before serving.
4. **Serve:**
    - Gently toss the salad to combine, or serve it in layers, with the dressing on the side.
    - Serve immediately to enjoy the freshness of the salad.

Tips:

- **Beets:** For easier peeling, you can rub the cooked beets with a paper towel or use a vegetable peeler.
- **Nuts:** Toasting the nuts enhances their flavor and crunch. Simply toast them in a dry skillet over medium heat for a few minutes until fragrant.
- **Cheese:** If you prefer a milder cheese, you can substitute goat cheese with feta cheese.
- **Make Ahead:** The roasted beets can be prepared ahead of time and stored in the refrigerator for up to 5 days. Assemble the salad just before serving to keep the greens fresh and crisp.

Roasted Beet and Goat Cheese Salad is a beautiful and delicious dish that combines sweet, savory, and tangy flavors. It's both nutritious and satisfying, making it a great addition to any meal. Enjoy!

Chicken Parmesan

Ingredients:

For the Chicken:

- 4 boneless, skinless chicken breasts
- 1 cup all-purpose flour
- 2 large eggs
- 1 cup breadcrumbs (plain or Italian seasoned)
- 1/2 cup grated Parmesan cheese
- 1 teaspoon dried Italian seasoning (optional)
- Salt and freshly ground black pepper, to taste
- 1 cup marinara sauce (store-bought or homemade)
- 1 1/2 cups shredded mozzarella cheese
- 1/4 cup chopped fresh basil or parsley (for garnish, optional)
- 2 tablespoons olive oil or vegetable oil (for frying)

For the Marinara Sauce (if homemade):

- 2 cups canned crushed tomatoes
- 1 tablespoon olive oil
- 1 small onion, finely chopped
- 2 cloves garlic, minced
- 1 teaspoon dried basil
- 1/2 teaspoon dried oregano
- Salt and freshly ground black pepper, to taste
- 1/4 teaspoon sugar (optional, to balance acidity)

Instructions:

1. **Prepare the Marinara Sauce (if homemade):**
   - Heat 1 tablespoon olive oil in a saucepan over medium heat.
   - Add the chopped onion and cook for 3-4 minutes until softened.
   - Stir in the minced garlic and cook for another 1 minute.
   - Add the crushed tomatoes, dried basil, dried oregano, salt, pepper, and sugar (if using).
   - Simmer the sauce for about 15-20 minutes, stirring occasionally, until it thickens. Adjust seasoning if needed. Set aside.
2. **Prepare the Chicken:**
   - Preheat your oven to 375°F (190°C).
   - Place each chicken breast between two pieces of plastic wrap or parchment paper. Pound the chicken with a meat mallet or rolling pin until it is about 1/2 inch thick.

- Set up a breading station: Place the flour in a shallow dish, beat the eggs in another shallow dish, and mix the breadcrumbs, grated Parmesan cheese, Italian seasoning (if using), salt, and pepper in a third shallow dish.
- Dredge each chicken breast in the flour, shaking off excess. Dip it in the beaten eggs, then coat it with the breadcrumb mixture, pressing gently to adhere.

3. **Fry the Chicken:**
   - Heat 2 tablespoons of olive oil or vegetable oil in a large skillet over medium heat.
   - Add the breaded chicken breasts and cook for 3-4 minutes per side, until they are golden brown and crispy. They do not need to be fully cooked through at this stage.
   - Transfer the fried chicken breasts to a paper-towel-lined plate to drain excess oil.

4. **Assemble and Bake:**
   - Spread a thin layer of marinara sauce in the bottom of a baking dish.
   - Place the fried chicken breasts on top of the sauce.
   - Spoon more marinara sauce over each chicken breast.
   - Sprinkle shredded mozzarella cheese evenly over the top.
   - Bake in the preheated oven for 20-25 minutes, or until the cheese is melted and bubbly, and the chicken reaches an internal temperature of 165°F (74°C).

5. **Garnish and Serve:**
   - Garnish with chopped fresh basil or parsley if desired.
   - Serve the Chicken Parmesan hot, with additional marinara sauce on the side if desired. It pairs well with pasta, a side salad, or garlic bread.

Tips:

- **Bread Crumbs:** For extra crunch, use panko breadcrumbs or a combination of breadcrumbs and crushed crackers.
- **Cheese:** If you prefer a more pronounced cheese flavor, use a mix of mozzarella and provolone.
- **Make-Ahead:** You can bread and fry the chicken ahead of time, then assemble and bake it just before serving.
- **Serving:** Serve with a simple side of spaghetti or a fresh green salad to round out the meal.

Chicken Parmesan is a comforting, satisfying dish that's perfect for a family dinner or special occasion. Enjoy the crispy, cheesy goodness!

Spaghetti Carbonara

Ingredients:

- 12 ounces spaghetti
- 2 tablespoons olive oil
- 4 ounces pancetta or guanciale (Italian cured pork), diced (or substitute with thick-cut bacon)
- 3 large eggs
- 1 cup grated Parmesan cheese (or Pecorino Romano for a sharper flavor)
- 2 cloves garlic, minced (optional)
- Freshly ground black pepper
- Salt, to taste
- Chopped fresh parsley (for garnish, optional)

Instructions:

1. **Cook the Spaghetti:**
    - Bring a large pot of salted water to a boil.
    - Add the spaghetti and cook according to the package instructions until al dente.
    - Reserve about 1 cup of pasta cooking water, then drain the spaghetti and set aside.
2. **Prepare the Pancetta:**
    - While the pasta is cooking, heat the olive oil in a large skillet over medium heat.
    - Add the diced pancetta (or guanciale) and cook until it becomes crispy and golden brown, about 5-7 minutes.
    - If using, add the minced garlic and cook for an additional 1 minute, until fragrant. Be careful not to burn the garlic.
    - Remove the skillet from the heat and set aside.
3. **Make the Carbonara Sauce:**
    - In a medium bowl, whisk together the eggs and grated cheese until well combined.
    - Season with freshly ground black pepper.
4. **Combine Pasta and Sauce:**
    - Add the drained spaghetti to the skillet with the pancetta, tossing to coat the pasta in the rendered fat.
    - Let the pasta cool slightly for a minute or two, which helps prevent the eggs from scrambling when added.
    - Gradually pour the egg and cheese mixture over the pasta, tossing continuously to coat the spaghetti evenly. The residual heat from the pasta will cook the eggs gently, creating a creamy sauce.
    - If the sauce is too thick, gradually add some of the reserved pasta cooking water, a little at a time, until you reach your desired consistency.
5. **Serve:**

- Serve the Spaghetti Carbonara immediately, garnished with additional grated cheese, freshly ground black pepper, and chopped parsley if desired.

Tips:

- **Pasta Water:** The reserved pasta water helps adjust the consistency of the sauce. It also adds a bit of starch to help the sauce cling to the pasta.
- **Eggs:** Ensure the pasta is not too hot when adding the egg mixture to prevent scrambling. The heat should be off or very low to gently cook the eggs into a creamy sauce.
- **Cheese:** Use good-quality Parmesan or Pecorino Romano cheese for the best flavor. Freshly grated cheese melts better than pre-grated cheese.
- **Meat:** Guanciale is traditional in Italian Carbonara, but pancetta or bacon is a common substitute. Ensure the meat is crispy to add texture to the dish.

Spaghetti Carbonara is a comforting and delicious pasta dish that's both elegant and easy to make. Enjoy the creamy, savory goodness of this Italian classic!

Cheese and Charcuterie Board

Ingredients:

Cheeses:

- **Hard Cheese:** Aged Gouda, Parmesan, or Manchego
- **Soft Cheese:** Brie, Camembert, or Goat Cheese
- **Blue Cheese:** Roquefort, Gorgonzola, or Stilton
- **Semi-Hard Cheese:** Cheddar or Gruyère

Charcuterie:

- **Cured Meats:** Prosciutto, Salami, or Soppressata
- **Pâté:** Chicken liver pâté or any gourmet pâté (optional)

Accompaniments:

- **Bread:** Crostini, baguette slices, or crackers
- **Fresh Fruits:** Grapes, apple slices, figs, or pear slices
- **Dried Fruits:** Apricots, raisins, or dates
- **Nuts:** Almonds, walnuts, or cashews
- **Pickles:** Gherkins, olives, or pickled onions
- **Condiments:** Honey, mustard, or fruit preserves (like fig jam)

Garnishes (optional):

- Fresh herbs (such as rosemary or thyme)
- Edible flowers

Instructions:

1. **Choose Your Board:**
   - Select a large wooden board, slate platter, or any serving tray. Ensure it has enough space to arrange all your ingredients attractively.
2. **Arrange the Cheeses:**
   - Place the cheeses on the board first. Space them out to allow room for accompaniments.
   - For each cheese, include a small knife or cheese spreader to make it easy for guests to serve themselves.
   - Cut some of the cheeses into slices or wedges, and leave others whole or in larger chunks.
3. **Add the Charcuterie:**
   - Arrange the cured meats around the cheeses. You can fold or roll slices for visual appeal.
   - If using pâté, place it in a small dish or spread it on the board.

4. **Incorporate Accompaniments:**
    - Place the bread, crackers, and any condiments in different sections of the board.
    - Arrange fresh and dried fruits, nuts, and pickles in gaps between the cheeses and meats. This adds color and texture.
5. **Garnish:**
    - Garnish the board with fresh herbs or edible flowers for a beautiful presentation.
6. **Serve:**
    - Provide small plates, forks, or toothpicks for easy serving.
    - If desired, include wine pairings or other beverages that complement the flavors of the board.

Tips:

- **Variety:** Aim for a mix of flavors and textures with your cheeses and meats. Including a variety of options ensures there's something for everyone.
- **Seasonal Ingredients:** Incorporate seasonal fruits and nuts to keep the board fresh and relevant to the time of year.
- **Presentation:** Arrange items in clusters rather than rows for a more natural and inviting look. Add height and variety by stacking or layering items.
- **Cheese Temperature:** Let cheeses sit at room temperature for about 30 minutes before serving to bring out their full flavor.

A Cheese and Charcuterie Board is all about variety and presentation. It's a versatile dish that can be customized to your preferences and those of your guests. Enjoy the delicious combinations and the art of creating an impressive board!

Chicken and Waffles

Ingredients:

For the Fried Chicken:

- 4 boneless, skinless chicken thighs (or breasts if preferred)
- 1 cup buttermilk
- 1 large egg
- 1 cup all-purpose flour
- 1 cup cornstarch
- 1 tablespoon paprika
- 1 teaspoon garlic powder
- 1 teaspoon onion powder
- 1 teaspoon dried thyme
- 1 teaspoon salt
- 1/2 teaspoon black pepper
- 1/2 teaspoon cayenne pepper (optional, for heat)
- Vegetable oil (for frying)

For the Waffles:

- 2 cups all-purpose flour
- 2 tablespoons sugar
- 1 tablespoon baking powder
- 1/2 teaspoon salt
- 1 3/4 cups milk
- 1/2 cup melted butter
- 2 large eggs
- 1 teaspoon vanilla extract

For Serving:

- Maple syrup
- Butter
- Fresh fruit (optional, such as berries or sliced bananas)
- Powdered sugar (optional)

Instructions:

1. **Prepare the Fried Chicken:**
    - In a large bowl, combine the buttermilk and egg. Add the chicken pieces and marinate in the refrigerator for at least 1 hour (or up to overnight for best results).
    - In a separate bowl, mix together the flour, cornstarch, paprika, garlic powder, onion powder, dried thyme, salt, pepper, and cayenne pepper.

- Heat about 1 inch of vegetable oil in a large skillet or deep fryer over medium-high heat to 350°F (175°C).
- Remove the chicken from the buttermilk, allowing excess to drip off. Dredge the chicken pieces in the flour mixture, pressing gently to coat well.
- Fry the chicken in batches, avoiding overcrowding the pan. Cook for about 6-8 minutes per side, or until golden brown and crispy, and the internal temperature reaches 165°F (74°C). Transfer the cooked chicken to a paper-towel-lined plate to drain.

2. **Make the Waffles:**
    - Preheat your waffle iron according to the manufacturer's instructions.
    - In a large bowl, whisk together the flour, sugar, baking powder, and salt.
    - In another bowl, mix the milk, melted butter, eggs, and vanilla extract.
    - Pour the wet ingredients into the dry ingredients and stir until just combined. Be careful not to overmix; it's okay if there are a few lumps.
    - Grease the waffle iron if needed and pour the batter onto the hot iron. Cook according to the waffle iron's instructions until the waffles are golden brown and crispy.
    - Keep the cooked waffles warm in a low oven (about 200°F or 95°C) while you cook the remaining waffles.

3. **Serve:**
    - Place a warm waffle on a plate and top with a piece of crispy fried chicken.
    - Drizzle with maple syrup and add a pat of butter if desired.
    - Garnish with fresh fruit or a dusting of powdered sugar if you like.

Tips:

- **Marination:** Marinating the chicken in buttermilk not only adds flavor but also helps to tenderize the meat and make the coating crispier.
- **Frying Temperature:** Ensure the oil is at the correct temperature to avoid greasy chicken. If the oil is too hot, the chicken will burn; if too cool, it will absorb too much oil.
- **Waffle Texture:** For extra crispy waffles, you can use a bit of cornstarch in the batter or replace some of the milk with buttermilk.
- **Serving:** For a more decadent touch, you can add a drizzle of honey along with the maple syrup.

Chicken and Waffles is a delightful fusion of flavors and textures, offering a savory and sweet combination that's sure to please. Enjoy this comforting dish for a special meal or a tasty treat!

Pork Schnitzel

Ingredients:

- 4 boneless pork loin chops or pork tenderloin, pounded thin
- 1/2 cup all-purpose flour
- 2 large eggs
- 1 cup breadcrumbs (plain or seasoned)
- 1/2 cup grated Parmesan cheese (optional)
- 1 teaspoon paprika (optional)
- Salt and freshly ground black pepper, to taste
- Vegetable oil or clarified butter (for frying)
- Lemon wedges (for serving)
- Fresh parsley, chopped (for garnish, optional)

Instructions:

1. **Prepare the Pork:**
   - If using pork loin chops, place each chop between two sheets of plastic wrap or parchment paper. Using a meat mallet or rolling pin, gently pound the pork until it is about 1/4 inch thick.
   - Season both sides of the pork with salt and pepper.
2. **Set Up the Breading Station:**
   - In one shallow dish, place the flour.
   - In a second shallow dish, beat the eggs.
   - In a third shallow dish, combine the breadcrumbs, Parmesan cheese (if using), paprika (if using), salt, and pepper.
3. **Bread the Pork:**
   - Dredge each pork cutlet in the flour, shaking off any excess.
   - Dip the floured pork into the beaten eggs, allowing any excess to drip off.
   - Coat the pork with the breadcrumb mixture, pressing gently to adhere and ensuring an even coating. Set the breaded cutlets aside on a plate.
4. **Fry the Schnitzels:**
   - Heat about 1/4 inch of vegetable oil or clarified butter in a large skillet over medium-high heat.
   - Once the oil is hot (but not smoking), add the breaded pork cutlets in batches, being careful not to overcrowd the pan.
   - Fry the schnitzels for 2-3 minutes per side, or until they are golden brown and crispy. Adjust the heat as needed to prevent burning.
   - Transfer the cooked schnitzels to a paper-towel-lined plate to drain excess oil.
5. **Serve:**
   - Serve the pork schnitzels hot with lemon wedges for squeezing over the top.
   - Garnish with chopped fresh parsley if desired.

Tips:

- **Pounding Pork:** Ensure the pork is pounded evenly to promote uniform cooking and to help it cook quickly.
- **Breading:** Press the breadcrumbs firmly onto the pork to ensure they adhere well during frying.
- **Oil Temperature:** Make sure the oil is hot enough to fry the schnitzels quickly, but not so hot that it burns the coating. If the oil is too cool, the schnitzels will become greasy.
- **Side Dishes:** Pork schnitzel pairs wonderfully with a variety of sides, such as potato salad, spaetzle, sauerkraut, or a simple green salad.

Pork Schnitzel is a flavorful, comforting dish that's perfect for a satisfying meal. Enjoy the crispy, golden schnitzels with your favorite accompaniments for a true taste of German cuisine!

Vegetable Stir-Fry

Ingredients:

For the Stir-Fry:

- 2 tablespoons vegetable oil (or any high-heat oil like canola or sesame oil)
- 1 medium onion, sliced
- 2 cloves garlic, minced
- 1 tablespoon fresh ginger, minced (or 1 teaspoon ground ginger)
- 1 red bell pepper, sliced
- 1 green bell pepper, sliced
- 1 cup broccoli florets
- 1 cup snap peas or snow peas
- 1 medium carrot, julienned or sliced thinly
- 1 cup mushrooms, sliced (button or shiitake work well)
- 1 zucchini, sliced (optional)
- 1 cup baby corn or regular corn kernels (optional)
- 2-3 green onions, sliced (for garnish)
- 1 tablespoon sesame seeds (for garnish, optional)

For the Sauce:

- 1/4 cup soy sauce (low-sodium preferred)
- 2 tablespoons hoisin sauce
- 1 tablespoon oyster sauce (or additional hoisin sauce for a vegetarian option)
- 1 tablespoon rice vinegar or apple cider vinegar
- 1 tablespoon brown sugar or honey
- 1 teaspoon cornstarch mixed with 2 tablespoons water (for thickening)
- 1/2 teaspoon crushed red pepper flakes (optional, for heat)

For Serving:

- Cooked rice or noodles
- Fresh cilantro or basil (for garnish, optional)

Instructions:

1. **Prepare the Vegetables:**
   - Wash and cut all vegetables into bite-sized pieces. Keep them in separate bowls for easy access.
2. **Make the Sauce:**
   - In a small bowl, whisk together the soy sauce, hoisin sauce, oyster sauce (or additional hoisin), rice vinegar, brown sugar or honey, and crushed red pepper flakes (if using). Mix the cornstarch with water to make a slurry and add it to the sauce. Set aside.
3. **Cook the Vegetables:**

- Heat 2 tablespoons of vegetable oil in a large skillet or wok over medium-high heat.
        - Add the sliced onion and cook for 2-3 minutes until softened.
        - Add the minced garlic and ginger, and cook for another 1 minute, until fragrant.
        - Add the broccoli, bell peppers, carrot, and snap peas. Stir-fry for 4-5 minutes until vegetables are tender-crisp.
        - Add the mushrooms, zucchini (if using), and baby corn (if using), and stir-fry for an additional 2-3 minutes.
    4. **Add the Sauce:**
        - Pour the prepared sauce over the vegetables. Stir well to coat all the vegetables.
        - Cook for another 1-2 minutes, until the sauce has thickened and the vegetables are well-coated.
    5. **Serve:**
        - Serve the vegetable stir-fry over cooked rice or noodles.
        - Garnish with sliced green onions, sesame seeds, and fresh herbs if desired.

Tips:

- **Vegetable Variety:** Feel free to customize the stir-fry with your favorite vegetables or whatever you have on hand. Just keep the cooking times in mind; add vegetables that take longer to cook first.
- **Prepping Ahead:** You can chop the vegetables and make the sauce ahead of time to make the cooking process quicker.
- **Heat Level:** Adjust the heat level of the dish by adding more or less crushed red pepper flakes to the sauce.
- **Protein Addition:** If you want to add protein, consider adding tofu, chicken, beef, or shrimp. Cook the protein first, then remove it from the pan and stir-fry it with the vegetables at the end.

Vegetable Stir-Fry is a quick and easy dish that's packed with flavor and nutrition. It's perfect for a busy weeknight or a healthy meal prep option. Enjoy!

Chicken Shawarma

Ingredients:

For the Chicken Marinade:

- 1 1/2 pounds boneless, skinless chicken thighs (or breasts if preferred)
- 1/4 cup plain yogurt
- 3 tablespoons olive oil
- 3 cloves garlic, minced
- 1 tablespoon ground cumin
- 1 tablespoon ground coriander
- 1 tablespoon ground paprika
- 1 tablespoon ground turmeric
- 1 tablespoon ground cinnamon
- 1 teaspoon ground allspice
- 1 teaspoon ground black pepper
- 1 teaspoon salt
- Juice of 1 lemon

For the Garlic Sauce:

- 1/2 cup mayonnaise
- 1/4 cup plain Greek yogurt
- 2 cloves garlic, minced
- 1 tablespoon lemon juice
- 1 tablespoon olive oil
- Salt and black pepper, to taste

For Serving:

- Pita bread or flatbreads
- Fresh vegetables (tomato slices, cucumber slices, red onion slices)
- Pickled vegetables (optional, such as pickled cucumbers or turnips)
- Fresh parsley or cilantro, chopped (for garnish)

Instructions:

1. **Marinate the Chicken:**
    - In a large bowl, combine the yogurt, olive oil, minced garlic, cumin, coriander, paprika, turmeric, cinnamon, allspice, black pepper, salt, and lemon juice.
    - Add the chicken thighs and toss to coat evenly with the marinade.
    - Cover and refrigerate for at least 1 hour, or preferably overnight for the best flavor.
2. **Cook the Chicken:**
    - Preheat your grill, grill pan, or oven broiler to high heat.
    - If grilling or using a grill pan, lightly oil the grates or pan.
    - Remove the chicken from the marinade and discard any excess marinade.

- Grill the chicken for about 5-7 minutes per side, or until the chicken is fully cooked and has a nice char, with an internal temperature of 165°F (74°C). Alternatively, broil the chicken on a baking sheet, flipping halfway through, for about 10-15 minutes total.
    - Let the cooked chicken rest for a few minutes before slicing it into thin strips.
3. **Prepare the Garlic Sauce:**
    - In a small bowl, mix together the mayonnaise, Greek yogurt, minced garlic, lemon juice, and olive oil.
    - Season with salt and black pepper to taste. Adjust the seasoning as needed.
4. **Assemble the Shawarma:**
    - Warm the pita bread or flatbreads slightly if desired.
    - Spread a generous amount of garlic sauce on the pita bread.
    - Add the sliced chicken on top of the sauce.
    - Top with fresh vegetables, pickled vegetables (if using), and chopped parsley or cilantro.
5. **Serve:**
    - Roll up the pita bread or flatbread around the fillings to create a wrap.
    - Serve immediately with extra garlic sauce on the side if desired.

Tips:

- **Marination Time:** For the best flavor, marinate the chicken for at least 1 hour, but overnight is ideal.
- **Cooking Options:** You can also bake the chicken at 400°F (200°C) for about 20-25 minutes, or until fully cooked.
- **Vegetable Options:** Feel free to add other fresh vegetables or toppings, such as shredded lettuce or radishes.
- **Make-Ahead:** The garlic sauce and marinated chicken can be made ahead of time for a quicker assembly.

Chicken Shawarma is a flavorful and versatile dish that's perfect for a delicious meal. Enjoy this Middle Eastern favorite with your favorite toppings and sides!

Cornbread and Chili Bake

Ingredients:

For the Chili:

- 1 lb (450g) ground beef (or ground turkey for a leaner option)
- 1 onion, finely chopped
- 2 cloves garlic, minced
- 1 bell pepper, chopped (red or green)
- 1 can (15 oz) kidney beans, drained and rinsed
- 1 can (15 oz) black beans, drained and rinsed
- 1 can (15 oz) diced tomatoes
- 1 cup beef or chicken broth
- 1 can (6 oz) tomato paste
- 2 tablespoons chili powder
- 1 teaspoon ground cumin
- 1 teaspoon smoked paprika
- 1/2 teaspoon dried oregano
- Salt and black pepper to taste
- 1 cup frozen corn kernels (optional)

For the Cornbread Topping:

- 1 cup all-purpose flour
- 1 cup cornmeal
- 1/4 cup granulated sugar
- 1 tablespoon baking powder
- 1/2 teaspoon salt
- 1 cup milk
- 1/4 cup vegetable oil or melted butter
- 1 large egg
- 1 cup shredded cheddar cheese (optional, for extra flavor)

Instructions:

1. **Prepare the Chili:**
   - In a large skillet or pot, cook the ground beef over medium heat until browned. Break it up into small pieces as it cooks.
   - Add the chopped onion, garlic, and bell pepper to the skillet and cook until the vegetables are softened, about 5 minutes.
   - Stir in the kidney beans, black beans, diced tomatoes, beef or chicken broth, tomato paste, chili powder, cumin, smoked paprika, oregano, salt, and pepper. Mix well.
   - Bring the mixture to a simmer and cook for about 15-20 minutes, until the chili has thickened. Stir in the frozen corn if using.
2. **Prepare the Cornbread Topping:**

- Preheat your oven to 400°F (200°C).
- In a large bowl, whisk together the flour, cornmeal, sugar, baking powder, and salt.
- In another bowl, mix the milk, vegetable oil (or melted butter), and egg until well combined.
- Pour the wet ingredients into the dry ingredients and stir until just combined. If using cheese, fold it into the batter.

3. **Assemble the Bake:**
   - Transfer the prepared chili into a greased 9x13-inch baking dish or similar oven-safe dish.
   - Spoon the cornbread batter evenly over the top of the chili. Smooth it out with a spatula if needed.

4. **Bake:**
   - Bake in the preheated oven for 20-25 minutes, or until the cornbread topping is golden brown and a toothpick inserted into the cornbread comes out clean.

5. **Serve:**
   - Allow the bake to cool slightly before serving. This helps the cornbread topping set and makes serving easier.
   - Serve hot, optionally garnished with sour cream, chopped green onions, or shredded cheese.

Tips:

- **Spice Level:** Adjust the chili powder and cumin to your preferred spice level. You can add a pinch of cayenne pepper for extra heat.
- **Cornbread Texture:** For a richer cornbread topping, you can substitute part of the milk with buttermilk.
- **Add-ins:** Feel free to add other vegetables to the chili, such as zucchini or mushrooms, or use different types of beans based on your preference.

Cornbread and Chili Bake is a satisfying and flavorful dish that brings together two classic comfort foods into one delicious meal. Enjoy this hearty bake for a family dinner or a cozy gathering with friends!

Grilled Portobello Mushrooms

Ingredients:

- 4 large Portobello mushrooms, stems removed and gills scraped out
- 1/4 cup olive oil
- 2 cloves garlic, minced
- 2 tablespoons balsamic vinegar
- 1 tablespoon soy sauce
- 1 tablespoon Dijon mustard
- 1 teaspoon dried thyme or rosemary (or 1 tablespoon fresh)
- 1 teaspoon paprika
- Salt and freshly ground black pepper, to taste
- Fresh parsley or basil, chopped (for garnish, optional)

Instructions:

1. **Prepare the Marinade:**
   - In a bowl, whisk together the olive oil, minced garlic, balsamic vinegar, soy sauce, Dijon mustard, dried thyme or rosemary, paprika, salt, and pepper.
2. **Marinate the Mushrooms:**
   - Place the Portobello mushrooms in a large resealable plastic bag or shallow dish.
   - Pour the marinade over the mushrooms, ensuring they are well coated. Seal the bag or cover the dish and let the mushrooms marinate in the refrigerator for at least 30 minutes. If you have more time, marinating for 1-2 hours will enhance the flavor.
3. **Preheat the Grill:**
   - Preheat your grill to medium-high heat. If using a gas grill, set it to medium-high. If using a charcoal grill, let the coals burn down until they are covered with a light layer of ash.
4. **Grill the Mushrooms:**
   - Remove the mushrooms from the marinade and shake off excess.
   - Place the mushrooms on the grill, gill side down. Grill for about 5-7 minutes on each side, or until they are tender and have nice grill marks. The mushrooms should be cooked through but still juicy.
5. **Serve:**
   - Remove the mushrooms from the grill and let them rest for a few minutes.
   - Garnish with chopped fresh parsley or basil if desired.
   - Serve the grilled Portobello mushrooms whole as a steak substitute or sliced over salads, pasta, or sandwiches.

Tips:

- **Marinating Time:** The longer you marinate the mushrooms, the more flavor they will absorb. If you're short on time, even a 30-minute marinade will add some flavor.
- **Grill Marks:** To get better grill marks, avoid moving the mushrooms too much while they're cooking.
- **Versatility:** You can also use this marinade for other vegetables or tofu.

Grilled Portobello Mushrooms are versatile, flavorful, and easy to prepare. They make a great addition to any meal, whether you're serving them as a main dish, side, or part of a larger spread.

Buffalo Cauliflower Bites

Ingredients:

For the Cauliflower Bites:

- 1 large head of cauliflower, cut into bite-sized florets
- 1 cup all-purpose flour (or use gluten-free flour if needed)
- 1 cup water (or milk for a richer batter)
- 1 teaspoon garlic powder
- 1 teaspoon onion powder
- 1 teaspoon paprika
- 1/2 teaspoon salt
- 1/2 teaspoon black pepper
- 1 cup breadcrumbs (plain or panko for extra crunch)
- 2 tablespoons olive oil or melted butter (for tossing the baked florets)

For the Buffalo Sauce:

- 1/2 cup hot sauce (such as Frank's RedHot)
- 2 tablespoons melted butter (or use olive oil for a dairy-free version)
- 1 tablespoon honey or maple syrup (optional, for a touch of sweetness)
- 1 teaspoon garlic powder (optional, for extra flavor)
- 1/2 teaspoon smoked paprika (optional, for extra smokiness)

For Serving:

- Ranch or blue cheese dressing (for dipping)
- Celery sticks or carrot sticks (for crunch and freshness)
- Fresh parsley, chopped (for garnish, optional)

Instructions:

1. **Prepare the Cauliflower:**
   - Preheat your oven to 450°F (230°C). Line a baking sheet with parchment paper or lightly grease it.
   - Cut the cauliflower into bite-sized florets.
2. **Make the Batter:**
   - In a large bowl, whisk together the flour, water (or milk), garlic powder, onion powder, paprika, salt, and pepper until smooth.
3. **Coat the Cauliflower:**
   - Dip each cauliflower floret into the batter, allowing any excess to drip off.
   - Roll the coated florets in the breadcrumbs until evenly coated.
   - Place the breaded cauliflower florets on the prepared baking sheet in a single layer.
4. **Bake the Cauliflower:**
   - Bake in the preheated oven for 20-25 minutes, or until the florets are golden brown and crispy. For extra crispiness, you can flip them halfway through baking.
5. **Prepare the Buffalo Sauce:**

- While the cauliflower is baking, mix together the hot sauce, melted butter, honey or maple syrup (if using), garlic powder, and smoked paprika in a small bowl.
6. **Toss the Cauliflower:**
    - Once the cauliflower is baked, remove it from the oven and place it in a large bowl.
    - Pour the buffalo sauce over the cauliflower and toss gently until all the florets are coated.
7. **Serve:**
    - Transfer the buffalo cauliflower bites to a serving platter.
    - Garnish with chopped fresh parsley if desired.
    - Serve with ranch or blue cheese dressing and celery or carrot sticks.

Tips:

- **Crispiness:** For extra crispy bites, you can spray a light coating of cooking spray over the breaded cauliflower before baking.
- **Buffalo Sauce Variations:** Adjust the amount of hot sauce based on your preferred spice level. For a milder version, use less hot sauce or add more honey/maple syrup.
- **Dairy-Free Option:** Use a dairy-free milk alternative in the batter and substitute olive oil for the butter in the buffalo sauce.

Buffalo Cauliflower Bites are a crowd-pleaser that offer the same tangy and spicy kick as traditional buffalo wings but with a healthier twist. Enjoy them as a game-day snack, party appetizer, or a fun addition to any meal!

Pasta Primavera

Ingredients:

For the Pasta:

- 12 ounces (340g) pasta (such as penne, fusilli, or spaghetti)
- Salt, for seasoning the pasta water

For the Vegetables:

- 2 tablespoons olive oil
- 1 medium onion, finely chopped
- 2 cloves garlic, minced
- 1 bell pepper (red, yellow, or orange), sliced
- 1 cup cherry tomatoes, halved
- 1 cup zucchini, sliced
- 1 cup broccoli florets
- 1 cup asparagus spears, trimmed and cut into bite-sized pieces
- 1 cup baby spinach or kale (optional)

For the Sauce:

- 1/2 cup vegetable or chicken broth
- 1/4 cup white wine (optional, or use additional broth)
- 1 tablespoon lemon juice
- 1 teaspoon dried oregano
- 1/2 teaspoon dried basil
- 1/4 teaspoon red pepper flakes (optional, for a bit of heat)
- Salt and freshly ground black pepper, to taste

For Garnish:

- 1/2 cup grated Parmesan cheese (or vegan cheese for a dairy-free option)
- Fresh basil or parsley, chopped (optional)

Instructions:

1. **Cook the Pasta:**
    - Bring a large pot of salted water to a boil.
    - Cook the pasta according to the package instructions until al dente.
    - Drain the pasta and set aside, reserving 1/2 cup of the pasta cooking water.
2. **Sauté the Vegetables:**
    - While the pasta is cooking, heat olive oil in a large skillet over medium heat.
    - Add the chopped onion and cook until softened, about 3-4 minutes.
    - Add the minced garlic and cook for another 1 minute until fragrant.
    - Add the bell pepper, cherry tomatoes, zucchini, broccoli, and asparagus. Cook, stirring occasionally, for about 5-7 minutes, or until the vegetables are tender but still crisp.

- If using baby spinach or kale, add it in the last minute of cooking and stir until wilted.
3. **Prepare the Sauce:**
   - Add the vegetable or chicken broth and white wine (if using) to the skillet. Bring to a simmer and cook for 2-3 minutes, allowing the liquid to reduce slightly.
   - Stir in the lemon juice, dried oregano, dried basil, and red pepper flakes (if using). Season with salt and pepper to taste.
4. **Combine Pasta and Vegetables:**
   - Add the cooked pasta to the skillet with the vegetables and sauce.
   - Toss to combine, adding a bit of the reserved pasta water if needed to help coat the pasta and vegetables with the sauce.
5. **Serve:**
   - Divide the Pasta Primavera among serving plates.
   - Sprinkle with grated Parmesan cheese and chopped fresh basil or parsley if desired.
   - Serve immediately.

Tips:

- **Vegetable Variations:** Feel free to use any vegetables you like or have on hand. Other great additions include mushrooms, snap peas, or artichoke hearts.
- **Vegan Option:** To make this dish vegan, omit the Parmesan cheese or use a dairy-free alternative.
- **Protein Addition:** For added protein, consider adding grilled chicken, shrimp, or tofu.

Pasta Primavera is a delicious and versatile dish that showcases the freshness of seasonal vegetables and is perfect for a light, yet satisfying meal. Enjoy the vibrant flavors and colorful presentation!

Honey Glazed Ham

Ingredients:

- 1 fully cooked bone-in ham (about 8-10 pounds)
- 1 cup honey
- 1/2 cup brown sugar
- 1/4 cup Dijon mustard
- 1/4 cup apple cider vinegar
- 1/4 cup orange juice
- 1/4 teaspoon ground cloves
- 1/4 teaspoon ground cinnamon
- 1/4 teaspoon black pepper

Instructions:

1. **Preheat Oven:** Preheat your oven to 325°F (163°C).
2. **Prepare the Ham:** Place the ham on a rack in a roasting pan. Score the surface of the ham in a diamond pattern, about 1/2 inch deep. This allows the glaze to penetrate the meat better.
3. **Make the Glaze:** In a saucepan, combine the honey, brown sugar, Dijon mustard, apple cider vinegar, orange juice, ground cloves, cinnamon, and black pepper. Cook over medium heat, stirring occasionally, until the mixture comes to a simmer and the sugar is dissolved. This should take about 5 minutes.
4. **Glaze the Ham:** Brush the ham generously with the glaze. Cover the ham loosely with aluminum foil.
5. **Bake the Ham:** Bake in the preheated oven for about 15-18 minutes per pound, or until the internal temperature reaches 140°F (60°C). Baste the ham with additional glaze every 20-30 minutes.
6. **Caramelize the Glaze:** For a nice caramelized finish, remove the foil during the last 30 minutes of baking. Brush the ham with more glaze and increase the oven temperature to 400°F (204°C). Bake, uncovered, until the ham is nicely caramelized.
7. **Rest and Serve:** Once done, remove the ham from the oven and let it rest for 15-20 minutes before carving. This allows the juices to redistribute throughout the meat.
8. **Serve:** Slice and serve with the remaining glaze.

Enjoy your honey glazed ham! It pairs wonderfully with sides like roasted vegetables, mashed potatoes, or a fresh salad.

Baked Brie with Cranberries

Ingredients:

- 1 round of Brie cheese (8 ounces)
- 1 cup cranberry sauce (store-bought or homemade)
- 1/4 cup chopped pecans (optional, for added crunch)
- 1 tablespoon honey (optional, for extra sweetness)
- Fresh rosemary or thyme (for garnish, optional)
- Crackers or slices of baguette (for serving)

Instructions:

1. **Preheat Oven:** Preheat your oven to 350°F (175°C).
2. **Prepare the Brie:** Place the round of Brie cheese on a parchment-lined baking sheet or in a small oven-safe dish.
3. **Top with Cranberries:** Spoon the cranberry sauce over the top of the Brie. You can use store-bought cranberry sauce, or make your own with fresh or frozen cranberries, sugar, and a bit of orange juice if you prefer.
4. **Add Pecans (Optional):** Sprinkle the chopped pecans on top of the cranberry sauce for added texture and flavor.
5. **Drizzle Honey (Optional):** Drizzle a little honey over the cranberries and nuts if you like a touch of extra sweetness.
6. **Bake:** Bake in the preheated oven for about 10-15 minutes, or until the Brie is soft and gooey in the center. The cranberry topping should be bubbly and slightly caramelized.
7. **Garnish:** If desired, garnish with fresh rosemary or thyme for a touch of color and a hint of herbal aroma.
8. **Serve:** Serve immediately with crackers, slices of baguette, or fresh fruit. It's best enjoyed warm when the Brie is melted and creamy.

Tips:

- **Homemade Cranberry Sauce:** If you want to make your own cranberry sauce, cook 12 ounces of fresh or frozen cranberries with 1 cup of sugar and 1/2 cup of water or orange juice until the cranberries burst and the sauce thickens (about 10 minutes). Let it cool before using.
- **Variations:** You can also add a layer of caramelized onions or a sprinkle of cinnamon for a unique twist.

This baked Brie with cranberries makes for a festive and crowd-pleasing appetizer that's perfect for gatherings, holidays, or a cozy night in. Enjoy!

Roasted Vegetable Tart

Ingredients:

For the Crust:

- 1 1/2 cups all-purpose flour
- 1/2 teaspoon salt
- 1/2 cup unsalted butter (cold and cut into small pieces)
- 1/4 cup ice water (more if needed)

For the Filling:

- **2 cups mixed vegetables** (e.g., bell peppers, zucchini, cherry tomatoes, red onion, eggplant)
- **2 tablespoons olive oil**
- **Salt and pepper** (to taste)
- **1/2 teaspoon dried thyme** or **rosemary** (or 1 teaspoon fresh herbs, chopped)
- **1/2 cup shredded cheese** (e.g., goat cheese, feta, or Gruyère)
- **3 large eggs**
- **1 cup heavy cream** or **half-and-half**
- **1/4 cup grated Parmesan cheese**
- **1 tablespoon fresh basil** or **parsley** (optional, for garnish)

Instructions:

1. **Preheat Oven:** Preheat your oven to 400°F (200°C).
2. **Prepare the Crust:**
   - In a food processor, combine the flour and salt. Add the cold butter and pulse until the mixture resembles coarse crumbs.
   - Gradually add the ice water, pulsing until the dough just comes together. You may need a little more or less water.
   - Turn the dough out onto a lightly floured surface, gather it into a ball, and then flatten into a disk. Wrap in plastic wrap and refrigerate for at least 30 minutes.
3. **Roast the Vegetables:**
   - Toss the mixed vegetables with olive oil, salt, pepper, and dried herbs. Spread them out on a baking sheet in a single layer.
   - Roast in the preheated oven for 20-25 minutes, or until the vegetables are tender and lightly caramelized. Let them cool slightly.
4. **Prepare the Tart Shell:**
   - On a lightly floured surface, roll out the chilled dough to fit a 9-inch tart pan. Transfer the dough to the pan, pressing it into the bottom and sides. Trim any excess.
   - Line the dough with parchment paper and fill with pie weights or dried beans. Bake in the preheated oven for 10 minutes. Remove the parchment and weights and bake for an additional 5 minutes, or until lightly golden. Let it cool slightly.
5. **Prepare the Filling:**

- In a bowl, whisk together the eggs, heavy cream, and grated Parmesan cheese. Season with a pinch of salt and pepper.
- Sprinkle the shredded cheese evenly over the pre-baked tart shell. Arrange the roasted vegetables on top of the cheese. Pour the egg mixture over the vegetables.

6. **Bake the Tart:**
    - Bake in the oven for 30-35 minutes, or until the filling is set and the top is golden brown.
7. **Garnish and Serve:**
    - Let the tart cool slightly before removing it from the pan. Garnish with fresh basil or parsley if desired.
    - Serve warm or at room temperature.

This roasted vegetable tart is versatile, so feel free to use your favorite vegetables or whatever is in season. It's perfect as a light main dish or a savory side. Enjoy!

Beef and Broccoli Stir-Fry

Ingredients:

For the Beef Marinade:

- 1/2 pound (225g) flank steak or sirloin (thinly sliced against the grain)
- 2 tablespoons soy sauce
- 1 tablespoon oyster sauce (optional)
- 1 tablespoon cornstarch
- 1 tablespoon rice wine or dry sherry (optional)
- 1 teaspoon sesame oil

For the Stir-Fry:

- 2 tablespoons vegetable oil
- 3 cups broccoli florets (fresh or frozen)
- 1 red bell pepper (sliced, optional)
- 2 cloves garlic (minced)
- 1 teaspoon fresh ginger (minced or grated)
- 1/4 cup soy sauce
- 2 tablespoons oyster sauce (optional)
- 2 tablespoons hoisin sauce (optional)
- 1 tablespoon cornstarch (mixed with 2 tablespoons water to make a slurry)
- 1/2 cup beef broth or water
- 1 teaspoon sesame oil
- Cooked rice or noodles (for serving)
- Sesame seeds (for garnish, optional)
- Chopped green onions (for garnish, optional)

Instructions:

1. **Marinate the Beef:**
   - In a bowl, combine the soy sauce, oyster sauce (if using), cornstarch, rice wine (if using), and sesame oil. Add the sliced beef and toss to coat. Let it marinate for at least 15 minutes, or up to 1 hour in the refrigerator.
2. **Prepare the Stir-Fry Sauce:**
   - In a small bowl, mix together the soy sauce, oyster sauce (if using), hoisin sauce (if using), and beef broth or water. Set aside.
3. **Blanch the Broccoli:**
   - Bring a pot of water to a boil. Add the broccoli florets and cook for 1-2 minutes until bright green and slightly tender. Drain and immediately transfer to a bowl of ice water to stop the cooking process. Drain again and set aside.
4. **Cook the Beef:**
   - Heat 1 tablespoon of vegetable oil in a large skillet or wok over medium-high heat. Add the marinated beef and stir-fry for 2-3 minutes, or until browned and just cooked through. Remove the beef from the skillet and set aside.
5. **Stir-Fry the Vegetables:**

- In the same skillet, add the remaining 1 tablespoon of vegetable oil. Add the garlic and ginger, and cook for about 30 seconds until fragrant.
- Add the broccoli (and bell pepper, if using) and stir-fry for 2-3 minutes until heated through and slightly tender.

6. **Combine Everything:**
   - Return the cooked beef to the skillet. Pour in the prepared stir-fry sauce and stir to combine.
   - Bring the mixture to a simmer and add the cornstarch slurry (cornstarch mixed with water). Stir continuously until the sauce thickens, about 1-2 minutes.
   - Drizzle with sesame oil and mix well.

7. **Serve:**
   - Serve the beef and broccoli stir-fry over cooked rice or noodles.
   - Garnish with sesame seeds and chopped green onions, if desired.

Enjoy your homemade beef and broccoli stir-fry! It's a satisfying and flavorful meal that's sure to be a hit at your dinner table.

Cajun Shrimp and Grits

Ingredients:

For the Grits:

- 1 cup stone-ground grits (or quick-cooking grits, but stone-ground is preferred)
- 4 cups water (or chicken broth for extra flavor)
- 1 cup milk (whole or 2%)
- 1/2 cup shredded sharp cheddar cheese (optional, for extra creaminess)
- 2 tablespoons unsalted butter
- Salt and black pepper (to taste)

For the Cajun Shrimp:

- 1 pound large shrimp (peeled and deveined)
- 2 tablespoons Cajun seasoning
- 1 tablespoon olive oil
- 1 tablespoon unsalted butter
- 3 cloves garlic (minced)
- 1/4 cup chicken broth
- 1 tablespoon lemon juice (fresh)
- Chopped green onions (for garnish, optional)
- Chopped parsley (for garnish, optional)

Instructions:

1. **Prepare the Grits:**
   - In a large pot, bring the water (or chicken broth) to a boil. Gradually whisk in the grits, reducing the heat to low.
   - Cover and cook, stirring occasionally, until the grits are thick and tender. This should take about 20-30 minutes for stone-ground grits or according to the package instructions for quick-cooking grits.
   - Once the grits are cooked, stir in the milk, cheddar cheese (if using), and butter. Season with salt and black pepper to taste. Keep warm on low heat while you prepare the shrimp.
2. **Prepare the Cajun Shrimp:**
   - In a medium bowl, toss the shrimp with the Cajun seasoning until evenly coated.
   - Heat the olive oil and butter in a large skillet over medium-high heat. Once the butter is melted and the oil is hot, add the seasoned shrimp.
   - Cook the shrimp for about 2-3 minutes on each side, or until they are pink and opaque. Be careful not to overcook the shrimp.
   - Add the minced garlic to the skillet and cook for another 1 minute, or until fragrant.
   - Pour in the chicken broth and lemon juice, and stir to combine. Let it simmer for another 1-2 minutes to slightly reduce the sauce.
3. **Serve:**
   - Spoon the creamy grits onto plates or into bowls.
   - Top with the Cajun shrimp and spoon some of the pan sauce over the top.

- Garnish with chopped green onions and parsley if desired.

Tips:

- **Make it Spicy:** Adjust the amount of Cajun seasoning to suit your spice preference. You can also add a pinch of cayenne pepper for extra heat.
- **Grits Consistency:** If the grits get too thick while sitting, you can thin them out with a bit more milk or water.

This dish is a wonderful blend of creamy, cheesy grits with spicy, savory shrimp, making it a favorite for many. Enjoy your Cajun Shrimp and Grits!

www.ingramcontent.com/pod-product-compliance
Lightning Source LLC
LaVergne TN
LVHW081603060526
838201LV00054B/2044